A
BRONTË
DIARY

A
BRONTË
DIARY

A Chronological History of the
Brontë Family
from 1775 to 1915

BY
MICHAEL STEED

Dalesman Books • 1990

The Dalesman Publishing Company Ltd,
Clapham, Lancaster, LA2 8EB

First published 1990

ISBN: 0 85206 993 6

Printed by Peter Fretwell & Sons,
Goulbourne Street, Keighley, West Yorkshire BD21 1PZ

Contents

INTRODUCTION

The purpose of this book is not to provide yet another Brontë biography - there are enough of those already - but to provide a quick reference as to what each member of the family was doing at any particular time. Not every available date, particularly with regard to the youthful paintings and writings, is included, as this book is intended to give an impression of what they were doing, not a complete catalogue.

The idea for this book came about as a result of a need; I had to remind myself of the activities of the Brontë family when reading one or other of the biographies and, although the book should be of interest to the casual reader, this in fact is its principal purpose. At the rear of the book can be found a 'Who's Who'. A number of names are mentioned through the book about whom little or no explanation is given. Where this happens the reader should consult the 'Who's Who' for a short description of that person.

Finally, I have tried to be as precise as possible with the dates, although occasionally I have had to make educated guesses when the precise date is not known. This book, however, is primarily intended as an aide-memoire and not as the last word on the activities of the Brontë family.

ACKNOWLEDGEMENTS

I would like to acknowledge the help given to me by many members of the Council of the Brontë Society, who gave up their time to examine my manuscript for errors and to come up with suggested improvements, particularly to Jocelyn Kellet who was the first to read it and encourage me to pursue it, and to Christine Sumner whose enthusiasm for its publication is largely responsible for its reaching a wider public.

I must also thank those writers whose original research into the history of this remarkable family has enabled me to put a chronological history together in this form.

My thanks are also due to Debbie, who has spent much time typing, re-typing and copying this book as it has gone through its various stages, and lastly, and by no means least, to my wife Laraine, who for many years now has accepted the fact that she has to share me with three sisters.

1775

Hugh Brunty working at a lime kiln at Mount Pleasant, County Down, meets and falls in love with Eleanor (Alice) McClory, sister of Paddy McClory, one of his workmates.

After losing his job, Hugh works for a farmer, James Harshaw of Donoughmore (see 1792).

1776

Hugh Brunty and Eleanor (Alice) McClory run away and are married at Magherally Church, County Down. They spend their honeymoon at Warrenpoint.

Hostility to the marriage as Hugh was Protestant and Eleanor Catholic, but the marriage was eventually accepted by the rest of the family.

2 Dec. Birth of Elizabeth Branwell (Aunt Branwell) at Penzance.

1777

17 Mar. Birth of Patrick Brontë (Brunty) at Emdale in the Parish of Drumballyroney, County Down (first of ten children).

1778

Hugh and Eleanor Brunty move with Patrick to Lisnacreevy.

24 Dec. Birth of Rev. Samuel Redhead (see 1819).

1783

15 Apr. Birth of Maria Branwell at Penzance, Cornwall.

Ruins of a two-roomed cottage at Emdale in Drumballyroney parish, County Down, where Patrick Brontë (Brunty) was born in 1777. A commemorative plaque was unveiled here by Phyllis Bentley in 1956. *(Chris Sumner)*

Drumballyroney Church, where Patrick preached his first-ever sermon in 1806. *(Chris Sumner)*

1787

Patrick hears John Wesley preach.

1789

25 June   John Wesley stays with William Tighe at 'Rosanna', County Wicklow. (Half Brother of Rev. Thomas Tighe - see 1798). This was Wesley's last visit to Ireland.

Autumn   Patrick commences work as a part time assistant to the local blacksmith.

1790

Patrick goes to work as an apprentice to a linen weaver, Robert Donald.

Marriage of John Fennell and Jane Branwell at Penzance.

1791

15 Apr.   Maria Branwell, aged 8, finishes her sampler.

9 Oct.   Jane Branwell Fennell born at Penzance.

Death of John Wesley.

1792

Patrick meets the Rev. Andrew Harshaw, receives lessons in the classics and mathematics and has the use of the library (see James Harshaw, kinsman, 1776).

Spring   Patrick goes to work with a linen draper called Clibborn in Banbridge.

10 June   Birth of Margaret Wooler at Rouse Mill, Batley - later she became Charlotte's headmistress and friend.

1793

Patrick obtains a position as a teacher at Glascar Hill Presbyterian School under the Rev. Alexander Moore, after the death of his employer Mr. Clibborn.

1794

The Brunty family move to Ballynaskeagh.

1795

Patrick's first experiments with name changes. He writes 'Pruty', 'Prunty' and 'Brunty' inside an arithmetic book.

1797

2 Jan.   Birth of Elizabeth Firth at Kipping House, Thornton.

1798

Patrick goes to teach at a school at Drumballyroney and becomes tutor to the children of the Rev. Thomas Tighe.

1800

Birth of William Smith Williams.

1802

Mr. Firth makes a gift of £200 to the living of Thornton.

Spring   Patrick able to have saved up £25.

12 June   Birth of Harriet Martineau at Norwich.

Summer   Patrick leaves the school at Drumballyroney.

Sept.   Patrick sails to England for university, thanks to the influence of the Rev. Thomas Tighe.

Exterior and interior views of the school at Drumballyroney where Patrick Brontë was a teacher. *(J. Glen; Chris Sumner)*

1 Oct.	Patrick enters St. John's College, Cambridge and registers as 'Patrick Branty'.
3 Oct.	Patrick returns to the Registrar and changes his entry to 'Patrick Bronte'.

1803

Feb.	Patrick obtains a Hare exhibition for £6.13.4 p.a. which he holds until 1806.
29 Mar.	Birth of Nancy Garrs at Bradford.
Dec.	Patrick obtains a Duchess of Suffolk exhibition for £1.3.4. p.a. which he holds until 1807.

1804

Feb.	Patrick awarded £20 p.a. from the Church Missionary Society - £10 each from Henry Thornton and William Wilberforce.
	He is influenced by Rev. Charles Simeon, who had been trained by Rev. John Fletcher, a friend of Wesley (see 1809).
13 July	Birth of Claire Zoe Parent (Mdme. Heger).

1805

June	Patrick obtains a Dr. Goodman exhibition for £1.17.6 p.a. which he holds until 1806.

1806

23 Apr. (Wed.)	Patrick receives his B.A.
9 June (Sun.)	Patrick's intention to offer himself for Holy Orders is displayed at All Saints Church, Cambridge.

4 July (Fri.)	Patrick applies to the Bishop of London as a candidate for Holy Orders.
Aug.	Patrick goes to London and stays for the first time at the Chapter Coffee House, Paternoster Row.
10 Aug. (Sun.)	Patrick ordained Deacon at Fulham Chapel.
Late *Sept.*	Patrick goes home to Ireland for a visit and preaches, without notes, his first ever sermon at Drumballyroney Church.
Oct.	Patrick moves to a curacy at Wethersfield, Essex at a stipend of £60 p.a. He lodges at the home of a Miss Mildred Davy and forms an association with her niece, Mary Burder.
12 Oct. (Sun.)	Patrick performs his first marriage ceremony.

1807

13 Mar.	William Brown is appointed sexton at Haworth Church.
1 July	Patrick offers himself for ordination as priest.
July	Patrick relieves for 3 weeks at Colchester.
July	Maria Branwell in Penzance is given or buys a copy of the book 'An Extract of the Christian's Pattern' by Thomas a Kempis (see 1826).
21 Dec.	Patrick ordained priest at the Chapel Royal of St. James, Westminster, by the Bishop of Salisbury.

1808

5 Apr.	Death of Thomas Branwell (Maria's father) in Penzance.
Aut.	Patrick relieves for a few weeks at St. Peter's Church, Glenfield, Leicestershire. He is offered but declines the curacy there.

Above: **Dewsbury Parish Church, where Patrick Brontë became curate in 1809.** *(Chris Sumner collection)*

Left: **25 Chapel Street, Penzance — the last home of Maria Branwell before coming north.** *(Chris Sumner)*

1809

1 Jan.	Patrick conducts his last service - a funeral - at Wethersfield Church.
7 Jan. (Sat.)	Patrick leaves Wethersfield to be assistant curate at All Saints Church, Wellington, Shropshire. There he meets his fellow curate, William Morgan, also John Fennell, at that time the Headmaster of a boarding school at Wellington and Mary Fletcher, widow of the Rev. John Fletcher of Madeley, appointed by Wesley as his successor. After Fletcher's death, Wesley appointed William Grimshaw of Haworth as his successor.
10 July	Birth of Constantin Heger in Brussels.
4 Dec.	Patrick leaves Wellington to be curate at All Saints Church, Dewsbury, Yorkshire, under Rev. John Buckworth, very much with the support of Mary Fletcher. The West Riding of Yorkshire was considered to be the centre of the Wesleyan revival.
5 Dec. (Tues.)	Patrick arrives at Dewsbury and lives at the vicarage.
11 Dec. (Mon.)	Patrick officiates at his first service at Dewsbury - the wedding of John Senior and Ellen Popplewell.
19 Dec.	Death of Anne Branwell (nee Carne), Maria Branwell's mother, at Penzance.
	Benjamin Branwell (Maria's brother) Mayor of Penzance.

1810

	Publication of Patrick's first work, "Winter - Evening Thoughts. A Miscellaneous Poem."
Spring	Patrick rescues a boy from drowning in the River Calder.
Whitsun Tues.	Patrick leads the annual Whitsun walk to the village of Earlsheaton for 'the sing' and is accosted by a drunken bully who Patrick throws down.

17

6 June	Patrick writes to the Secretary of the York Diocese asking for the curacy of Hartshead-cum-Clifton.
Early Summer	Patrick leaves the vicarage and takes lodgings at the Ancient Well-House, Priests Lane.
19 July	Rev. John Buckworth, vicar of Dewsbury, writes to the Archbishop of York recommending Patrick for the curacy of Hartshead.
20 July	Patrick licensed to the curacy at Hartshead, but is unable to leave Dewsbury, forgets to read himself in and another cleric takes duty there.
20 Sept.	Wrongful arrest for desertion of William Nowell and first attempts by Patrick to overturn his committal.
29 Sept.	Birth of Elizabeth Cleghorn Stephenson (Mrs. Gaskell).
End of Nov.	Patrick finally obtains release of William Nowell, having involved the assistance of Viscount Milton, William Wilberforce and Lord Palmerston.

1811

Publication of Patrick's book 'Cottage Poems'. The title page shows Brontë, although Patrick continued usually to spell his name Bronte until after Charlotte became famous. His children would always use the diaeresis.

Jan. / Feb.	Incident involving Patrick and Rev. Buckworth's father in law, Mr. Halliley, resulting in Patrick refusing to preach again in Dewsbury Parish Church. Mr. Halliley, referring to Patrick, had said "Why keep a dog and bark yourself."
3 Mar.	Patrick moves to a curacy at Hartshead, 5 miles from Dewsbury. On his move the Rev. Buckworth presents him with his own book of sermons.
11 Mar.	Patrick signs the register at Dewsbury Parish Church for the last time.
Early April	William Morgan (see 1809 and later) becomes curate to John Crosse at Bradford and minister at Bierley Chapel

where the patron was Miss Frances Mary Richardson Currer.

11 June Patrick writes his comic poem 'Tweed's letter to his Mistress.' Tweed being the Buckworth's dog.

20 July Patrick officially inducted as minister at St. Peters Church, Hartshead, Liversedge. He lodges with a Mr & Mrs Bedford at Lovsey Thorn, Hightown, Liversedge.

Winter Luddite problems in the area.

1812

8 Jan. Wesleyan Academy at Woodhouse Grove opens, originally for eight pupils (seventy by 1813). John Fennell (see 1809 and later) is appointed First Master.

Feb. Luddites destroy machines over Hartshead Moor.

Spring Patrick appointed an examiner at Woodhouse Grove.

11 / 12 Apr. Luddite attack on William Cartwright's Rawfolds Mill at Liversedge and receive their first defeat (later used in 'Shirley').

c15 Apr. Patrick alleged to have discovered Luddites burying bodies in the graveyard at Hartshead Church but does nothing.

28 Apr. Murder of William Horsfall by the Luddites on Crossland Moor.

11 May Spencer Perceval, the Prime Minister, is assassinated at the House of Commons.

June Patrick meets Maria Branwell, who is staying at Woodhouse Grove School.

Aug. Patrick conducts oral examinations at Woodhouse Grove.

26 Aug. Probably Maria Branwell's first letter to Patrick.

End Aug. / Sept. Patrick proposes to and is accepted by Maria Branwell whilst on a visit to the ruins of Kirkstall Abbey.

Nineteenth-century engravings of
Kirkstall Abbey, which Patrick Brontë
and Maria Branwell visited in 1812.

5 Sept.	Maria Branwell and her cousin Jane Fennell go to Calverley Church to hear the Rev. Watman preach.
10 Sept.	Maria Branwell spends the day at Mire Shay, an old Jacobean building near Bradford.
16 Sept.	Maria Branwell, Patrick Brontë, Jane Fennell and William Morgan visit Kirkstall Abbey. This may have been when Patrick proposed.
17 Sept. (Thurs.)	Maria Branwell writes to her sisters in Penzance to tell them of her engagement.
7 Oct.	Patrick stays at Woodhouse Grove.
8 Oct.	Patrick, Maria Branwell, Jane Fennell and William Morgan visit Kirkstall Abbey.
24-27 Oct.	Maria Branwell and Jane Fennell visit Bradford.
14 Nov.	Maria Branwell hears of the shipwreck resulting in the loss of most of her personal belongings being sent by her sister from Penzance.
22 Nov.	Patrick visits William Morgan at Bierley and Woodhouse Grove in the evening.
23 or 24 Nov.	Patrick, Maria Branwell, Jane Fennell and William Morgan go to Leeds.
26 Dec.	Patrick sells two trees from his parsonage, Clough House, Hightown, to a Thomas Milnes for 3 guineas. Patrick is said to have been short of money.
29 Dec.	Marriage of Patrick to Maria Branwell at Guiseley Church conducted by William Morgan.
	Marriage of William Morgan to Jane Fennell at Guiseley Church conducted by Patrick Brontë. Both brides given away by John Fennell.
	Marriage of Maria's sister, Charlotte Branwell, to her cousin Joseph Branwell of Penzance.

St. Peter's Church at Hartshead, near Liversedge. Patrick Brontë was officially inducted as minister here in 1811. *(J. Kempson)*

Guiseley Parish Church, where Patrick and Maria Branwell were married on December 29th, 1812. *(Chris Sumner)*

Interior view of Hartshead Church. *(Gordon Hopper)*

1813

Publication of Patrick's 'The Rural Minstrel'.

John Fennell leaves Woodhouse Grove School.

Jan.   Patrick and Maria set up home at Clough House, Hightown, Liversedge.

15 Apr.   Maria's birthday for which Patrick writes the poem 'Lines addressed to a Lady on her Birthday'.

1814

Early Jan.   Birth of Maria Brontë at Hightown, Liversedge.

15 Apr.   Mr. Firth (see 1815 and onwards) thrown out of his gig but not seriously hurt.

23 Apr.   Maria christened by William Morgan with himself and his wife Jane and Mrs. Fennell as godparents.

29 May   Christening of William Weightman at Appleby (see 1839 and onwards).

2 July   Mrs. Firth is thrown out of her gig outside her home in Thornton and is killed.

Autumn   Rev. Thomas Atkinson of Thornton suggests to Patrick that they exchange livings as he wants to be nearer his fiancee, Frances Walker, of Lascelles Hall, Kirkheaton, Huddersfield.

1815

8 Feb. (Wed.)   Birth of Elizabeth Brontë at Hightown.

13 Mar.   Patrick's first official duties at Thornton, although still at Hartshead.

15 May   Patrick's last officiation at Hartshead Church.

19 May   Patrick exchanges living at Hartshead for Thornton.

7 June	First visit by Elizabeth Firth to the Brontës.
9 June	First meeting between Elizabeth Firth and Maria and Elizabeth.
Early June	Maria's sister Elizabeth Branwell of Penzance, goes to stay with the Brontës (Aunt Branwell).
June	Defeat of Napoleon at Waterloo by the Duke of Wellington.
12 June	First visit of Mrs. Maria Brontë and Miss Elizabeth Branwell to Elizabeth Firth.
23 July	A collection is made at Patrick's church, the Old Bell Chapel, for the widows and orphans of those who fell at Waterloo.
26 Aug.	Elizabeth is christened by John Fennell with Elizabeth Firth, Mr. Firth and Elizabeth Branwell as godparents.

1815

6 Sept.	Mr. Firth is remarried - to a Miss Greave.
9 Dec.	Death of Mary Fletcher of Madeley (see 1809).
	Publication of Patrick's 'The Cottage in the Wood'.

1816

29 Mar.	Patrick gives a signed copy of his 'Cottage Poems' to Elizabeth Branwell.
21 Apr. (Sun.)	Birth of Charlotte Brontë at Thornton.
May	Mr. Firth seriously ill but recovers.
29 June	Charlotte christened by William Morgan with Thomas Atkinson, Frances Walker (see 1814) and probably Charlotte Branwell as godparents.

The house on Market Street, Thornton, where Charlotte, Branwell, Emily and Anne Brontë were born. *(J. Kempson)*

7 July	Patrick preaches at William Morgan's new church, Christ Church, Bradford.
July	Nancy Garrs taken on as house servant by the Brontës.
28 July (Sun.)	Elizabeth Branwell leaves Thornton and returns home to Penzance.
19 Nov.	An eclipse of the sun, observed by Miss Firth at the Brontë's home.

1817

26 Feb.	Birth of Mary Taylor (see 1831 and onward).
22 Apr.	Birth of Ellen Nussey (see 1831 and onward).
9 May	First visit for dinner of the Brontë children to the Firths.
13/14 May	Patrick and Mr. Firth go to Bradford.
June	The prose section of Patrick's 'Cottage In The Wood' appears in the Cottage magazine.
26 June (Thurs.)	Birth of Patrick Branwell Brontë at Thornton in the early hours of the morning.
23 July	Branwell christened by John Fennell with Mr & Mrs Firth and probably himself as godparents.
6 Nov.	Patrick and Elizabeth Firth go to Bradford.
12 Nov.	Patrick and Maria dine at the Firths and there meet Rev. Samuel Redhead (see 1819).

1818

Publication of Patrick's 'The Maid of Killarney'.

6 Jan. (Tues.)	Birth of Arthur Bell Nicholls at Killead, County Antrim (see 1845 and onward).

Feb.	Maria (mother) unwell.
March	Patrick walks 60 local children to Bradford and back through snow, to be confirmed and himself pays for them to have a hot dinner at the Talbot Hotel, Kirkgate, Thornton.
30 July (Thurs.)	Birth of Emily Jane Brontë at Thornton.
Summer	Repairs being carried out to the Old Bell Chapel.
Aug.	Sarah Garrs taken on by the Brontës as a children's nurse and Nancy Garrs promoted to cook and assistant housekeeper.
20 Aug.	Emily christened at St. James Church, Thornton by William Morgan with Mr & Mrs Fennell and their daughter Jane Morgan as godparents.
	Second edition of Patrick's 'The Cottage In The Wood' is published.

1819

8 Jan. (Fri.)	Maria, Elizabeth and Charlotte go to tea with Elizabeth Firth.
25 May	Death of Rev. James Charnock, incumbent at Haworth.
1 June	Patrick recommended for curacy at Haworth by Mr. M. Stocks to one of the trustees of Haworth Church, Mr. Greenwood.
2 June	Vicar of Bradford appoints Patrick as curate of Haworth but does not seek the Trustees' approval.
Early July	Because of objections to the manner of his appointment, Patrick visits Mr. Stephen Taylor, one of the Trustees.
14 July	On Taylor's advice, Patrick resigns the curacy.
c17 July	Trustees of Haworth suggest to the Vicar of Bradford that Patrick preaches in Haworth Church so that they can judge him.

21 July	Patrick refuses to be examined and says that the Trustees must come to Thornton to hear him.
4 Oct.	The Brontë children go to tea at the Firths.
8 Oct.	The Archbishop of York commands Patrick to preach at Haworth Church.
10 Oct.	Patrick preaches at Haworth Church for the first time.
21 Oct.	Patrick formally resigns the curacy of Haworth to the Vicar of Bradford.
25 Oct.	Vicar of Bradford appoints Rev. Samuel Redhead to Haworth, again without seeking Trustees' approval.
31 Oct. (Sun.)	Samuel Redhead officiates at Haworth Church and the whole congregation walks out.
7 Nov. (Sun.)	Samuel Redhead again officiates and a man wearing several old hats rides backwards up the aisle on an ass.
14 Nov. (Sun.)	Samuel Redhead again officiates and a chimney sweep covered in soot embraces him during the service. Rev. Redhead is then marched out of church, falls over several gravestones and eventually seeks refuge in the Black Bull Inn, later escaping a mob through the back door.
17 Nov. (Wed.)	Patrick signs the register at Haworth for the first time (a funeral) and is looking after both Haworth and Thornton until a decision is made about the curacy.

1820

17 Jan. (Mon.)	Birth of Anne Brontë at Thornton. The other children spend the day with Elizabeth Firth.
27 Jan.	Patrick writes to the Secretary of the Governor's Bounty Office at Westminster, asking for financial assistance for the Thornton living.
13 Feb.	Patrick's last christening at Thornton.

29

25 Feb.	Patrick is licensed to the Perpetual Curacy at Haworth after a compromise between the Vicar of Bradford and the Trustees.
25 Mar.	Anne is christened by William Morgan with Mr. Firth, Elizabeth Firth and Miss Fanny Outhwaite as godparents.
31 Mar.	Good Friday, but no service held at Thornton because of expected trouble from Luddites.
20 Apr. (Thurs.)	The Brontës move to Haworth.
21 Apr.	Patrick holds his first meeting of the parish council.
6 June	Patrick goes to Thornton to visit William Morgan and the Firths at Kipping House. Nancy Garrs had forgotten to clean his boots but he said nothing and walked all the way in slippers.
13 Dec.	Patrick visits Mr. Firth, who is ill, at Thornton.
21 Dec.	Patrick again visits Mr. Firth.
27 Dec.	Death of Mr. Firth.

1821

29 Jan.	Maria (mother) taken ill. Found collapsed.
9 Feb.	Elizabeth Firth visits the Brontës at Haworth. Mrs. Brontë described as 'very poorly'.
Apr.	All six children ill with scarlet fever.
	Patrick's 'The Maid of Killarney' appears in the Cottage Magazine.
Early May	Elizabeth Branwell comes to Haworth from Penzance because of her sister's illness.
26 May- 22 June	Maria and Elizabeth stay with Elizabeth Firth at Thornton.

31 May	Marriage of Robert Heaton of Ponden House (the Lintons of Thrushcross Grange in 'Wuthering Heights'?) to Alice Midgley of the Manor House, Haworth.
17 Aug.	Patrick dines with Elizabeth Firth at Thornton.
25 Aug.	Death in Ireland of Thomas Tighe (see 1798).
Sept.	Rev. William Anderton taking services at Haworth while Patrick stays with his wife.
15 Sept. (Sat.)	Death of Mrs. Maria Brontë of cancer.
22 Sept.	Funeral of Mrs. Maria Brontë.
23 Nov.	Patrick's old vicar, Rev. John Buckworth of Dewsbury, writes him a letter of condolence.
8/10 Dec.	Patrick stays with Elizabeth Firth at Kipping House, Thornton.
12 Dec.	Elizabeth Firth receives a letter from Patrick. Either during the visit or in the letter, Patrick proposes marriage and is rejected.
14 Dec.	Elizabeth Firth writes a 'last letter' to Patrick and on the same day her future husband, Rev. James Franks of Sowerby Bridge, comes to dinner.

1822

4 May	Birth of Robert Heaton - christened by Patrick Brontë.
25 July	Charlotte, aged 6, completes her sampler.
	Patrick proposes to Isabella Drury of Keighley and is refused.

1823

Patrick again appointed an examiner at Woodhouse Grove School.

Clough House, Hightown — Patrick and Maria set up home here in 1813.
(J. Kempson)

Cowan Bridge School, near Kirkby Lonsdale, attended by Maria, Elizabeth, Charlotte and Emily, which became the Lowood School of 'Jane Eyre'.

Roe Head School, Mirfield Moor, where Charlotte became a pupil in 1831. *(Chris Sumner)*

Heald's House, Dewsbury Moor. Miss Wooler's school after Roe Head, attended by Charlotte. *(Chris Sumner)*

Apr.- *July*	Correspondence between Patrick and Mary Burder and her mother (see 1806) at Wethersfield, Essex in which Patrick suggests a renewing of their relationship but is rejected.
8 Aug.	Final rejection letter to Patrick from Mary Burder.
	Maria and Elizabeth spend a few months at Crofton Hall School, Wakefield but too expensive so moved.
4-6 Oct.	Last visit of Patrick to Elizabeth Firth at Thornton.
Oct.	Elizabeth Firth gives Anne, her god-daughter, a bible.
Dec. / *Jan.*	Epidemics of measles, whooping cough and chicken pox at Haworth and all the children ill.

1824

1 Jan.	Patrick again writes to Mary Burder suggesting marriage.
Jan. / *Apr.*	All children continue to be ill with successive bouts of chicken pox, measles and whooping cough.
30 Jan.	The Clergy Daughters' School at Cowan Bridge near Tunstall, Lancashire, is opened by Rev. Carus Wilson. The Superintendent is Anne Evans - a kind woman. The decision is taken to send Maria and Elizabeth there, but this is delayed due to their illnesses.
Spring	Whole family ill with whooping cough.
27 Apr.	Elizabeth Firth leaves Kipping House, Thornton.
24 June	Patrick goes to Bradford and buys Branwell's birthday present of twelve soldiers for 1/6. These were not the soldiers which led to the stories of the Twelves (see 1826).
1 July	Maria and Elizabeth go to Cowan Bridge School - both still weak from their illness through the winter.
	Marriage of Mary Burder to the Rev. Peter Sibree of Wethersfield. She has four children.

10 Aug.	Charlotte joins Maria and Elizabeth at Cowan Bridge School. (She later describes the school and records her experiences there as Lowood School in 'Jane Eyre').
2 Sept. (Thurs.)	Huge landslip on the moors above Haworth witnessed by Branwell, Emily and Anne out walking with Nancy and Sarah Garrs.
12 Sept.	Patrick preaches a sermon on the landslip, which is later privately printed.
21 Sept.	Marriage of Elizabeth Firth to Rev. James Franks.
End Sept.	Whilst on her honeymoon Elizabeth Franks (Firth) calls at Cowan Bridge and gives Maria, Elizabeth and Charlotte half-a-crown each.
10 Nov.	Patrick writes to his banker Mr. Marrimer at Keighley, to say he is withdrawing £20 to send Emily to school.
25 Nov.	Emily joins her sisters at Cowan Bridge School.
Dec.	Nancy Garrs leaves the Parsonage to get married.

1825

Mechanics Institute, Keighley founded.

Jan.	Patrick's sermon on the Haworth Landslip (see 1824) is published in the Cottage Magazine.
Jan./ Feb.	Tabitha Aykroyd (Tabby) comes to the Parsonage as cook.
	Epidemic of low fever (typhoid) breaks out at Cowan Bridge School.
Feb.	Sarah Garrs leaves the Parsonage.
13 Feb.	Patrick is informed that Maria is very ill.
14 Feb. (Fri.)	Maria leaves Cowan Bridge for Haworth.
6 May	Death of Maria.

12 May	Maria Brontë's funeral conducted by William Morgan.
31 May	Elizabeth also ill and is sent home from Cowan Bridge. Charlotte and Emily are sent to the home of the Rev. Wilson (founder of the school) at Silverdale, Morecambe Bay.
1 June	Patrick collects Charlotte and Emily and takes them home.
	Birth of William Heaton, later christened by Patrick Brontë.
15 June	Death of Elizabeth.
18 June	Elizabeth Brontë's funeral, conducted by William Morgan.
25 Aug.	Patrick writes to the Bounty Office, Westminster for financial assistance.
23 Sept.	Patrick receives a refund of £12.2.4 from Cowan Bridge School because the children were removed.
1 Dec.	Patrick again writes to the Bounty Office but his request is denied.

1826

Early in Year	Charlotte writes her first story - for Anne, who was probably ill.
Feb.	Death of the Haworth Parish Clerk, Stephen Parslow.
29 May	The children recreate Oak Apple Day. Emily climbs into a cherry tree in the garden from Patrick's window, breaking off a branch. She and Tabby try and cover the bare patch with soot to hide it.
5 June	Patrick attends a clerical conference in Leeds and brings the children presents home. Ninepins for Charlotte, a toy village for Emily, a dancing doll for Anne and twelve toy soldiers for Branwell. These soldiers are given names by the children and become

the basis of the stories of the Twelves, and given imaginary countries, governments and social life.

June   Charlotte writes 'The Young Men' and the children create the Chief Genii - Branii, Tallii, Emmii and Annii.

July   Patrick gives Charlotte her mother's copy of 'An Extract of the Christian's Pattern' by Thomas a Kempis (see 1807).

4 Sept.   Charlotte sketches a thatched cottage for Anne.

1827

Feb.   Patrick gives Emily a Bible.

13 Feb.   Anne given a Book of Common Prayer by her godmother, Miss Outhwaite.

12 Mar.   Earliest known writing by Branwell - 'My Battell Book'.

22 Mar.   Birth of John Heaton, later christened by Patrick Brontë.

July   'Our Fellows' written by the children.

Branwell buys a set of Turkish musicians in Halifax.

24 Sept.   Death of Jane Morgan, aged 36. She is buried at Cross Stone Church, near Todmorden.

1 Dec.   Charlotte and Emily start their Bed Plays - probably secret plays made up in bed at night.

Dec.   'The Play of the Islanders' started by the children.

1828

Jan.   Elizabeth Branwell gives a three volume set of Scott's 'Tales of a Grandfather' to the children as a New Year present.

Apr.   Charlotte and Emily complete samplers.

17 May	Branwell sketches a tower and castle for Anne.
8 June	Birth of Martha Brown (see 1839).
28 July	Branwell completes a pencil drawing copy of a vignette by Beswick of a dog and cockrell fighting in a farmyard, and Charlotte a drawing of a stone wall.
29 Aug.	Ann sketches a tower with pine trees.
2 Sept.	Charlotte sketches a ruined tower and gate for Anne.
4 Sept.	Charlotte sketches a thatched cottage for Anne.
	Branwell buys a box of Indians in Haworth.
17 Nov.	Branwell sketches a round tower and castle for Anne.
28 Nov.	Anne completes a sampler.
	Branwell sketches a sleeping cat.

1829

First six volumes of 'The Young Men's Magazine' written by the children.

Jan.	First issue of Branwell's 'Blackwoods Magazine'.
7 Jan.	Emily sketches a window.
14 Jan.	Charlotte sketches a girl and a stone house.
15 Jan.	Patrick has a letter on Catholic emancipation published in the 'Leeds Intelligencer'. (Also on 29 Jan. and 5 Feb.).
24 Jan.	Charlotte sketches a bird on a rock in the sea.
23 Feb.	Branwell sketches a ruined tower and church for Anne.
1 Mar.	Emily finishes a sampler and copies a picture of a winchat from her father's book of 'Beswick's British Birds'.
12 Mar.	Charlotte writes her 'History of the Year 1829'.

Haworth Parsonage, and Haworth Church interior, as they were in the days of the Brontës.

2 Apr.	Charlotte finishes her 'The Twelve Adventurers' and 'The Adventurous Ireland' and Emily sketches a woman, birds and a farm.
7 Apr.	Anne sketches a cottage and trees.
23 Apr.	Anne sketches a bird and a toad.
25 Apr.	Emily draws a landscape with a woman and a goose.
May / June	Branwell starting to learn Greek.
18 May	Charlotte sketches a boy with a large dog.
22 May	Charlotte sketches trees and a girl with a baby, and Emily copies a picture of a ring ousel from her father's book of 'Beswick's British Birds'.
26 May	Death of Mrs. Fennell. She is buried at Cross Stone Church near Todmorden. Mrs. Fennell was Aunt Branwell's aunt.
	Charlotte sketches 'Revenante Castle'.
30 June	Charlotte commences 'Tales of the Islanders'.
6 July	Charlotte finishes 'Leisure Hours' and 'Two Fragments'.
13 July	Charlotte sketches 'The Keeper of the Bridge'.
20 July	Charlotte sketches the ruins of a palace.
Aug.	Charlotte changes Branwell's 'Blackwoods Magazine' to 'Blackwoods Young Men's Magazine' and edits it herself.
1 Aug.	Charlotte finishes 'The Search after Happiness'.
Sept.	Branwell writes his 'Young Soult's Poems'.
23 Sept.	Following the death of Mrs. Fennell, the children and Miss Branwell go to stay at the Parsonage, Cross Stone, near Todmorden.
25 Sept.	Children return to Haworth.

13 Nov.	Branwell is given a New Testament in Latin to study from.
Dec.	Branwell paints a portrait of himself and his three sisters. (The Gun Group).
17 Dec.	Charlotte finishes 'Characters of Great Men of the Present Age' and 'A Book of Rhymes'.

1830

23 Jan.	Anne completes a sampler.
2 Feb.	Charlotte finishes 'The Adventures of Edward de Crack'.
11 Feb.	Birth of Mary Anne Bell (see 1864).
11 Mar.	Charlotte paints a watercolour of 'The Mountain Sparrow'.
30 Apr.	Branwell paints a watercolour 'The Hermit'.
6 May	Patrick writes to the Leeds Intelligencer about the criminal code, and Branwell completes a watercolour of a man in a turban reading.
11 May	Branwell sketches 'Terror'.
26 May	Charlotte finishes 'The Adventures of Ernest Alembert'.
30 May	Charlotte finishes 'Miscellaneous Poems'.
10 June	Charlotte finishes 'An Interesting Incident in the Lives of Some of the Most Eminent Persons of the Age'.
22 June	An old man comes to see Patrick, who is ill in bed, and sees Tabby instead to give a message from 'the Lord' that 'the bridegroom is coming'.
26 June	Death of King George IV and accession of William IV and Queen Adelaide. (Emily named her two geese after Queen Adelaide and the Princess Victoria).

26-28 June	Branwell writes his play 'Caractacus A Dramatic Poem by Young Soult'.
12 July	Charlotte finishes 'The Poetaster'.
13 July	Charlotte completes a watercolour of wild roses.
15 July	Charlotte completes a watercolour of a girl and flowers.
30 July	Charlotte finishes her four volume story 'Tales of the Islanders' (started 30 June 1828).
3 Aug.	Charlotte compiles a catalogue of her books to date.
Aug.	Charlotte amends the name 'Blackwoods Young Men's Magazine' to 'Young Men's Magazine'.
Summer	Patrick seriously ill with congestion of the lungs and unable to perform his duties for six months (see also 22 June).
3 Sept.	Coronation of King William IV.
Oct.	Charlotte finishes 'Albion and Marina'.
	Elizabeth Branwell gives Mrs. Maria Brontë's portrait to Charlotte for her to copy.
15 Dec.	Branwell starts his 'History of the Young Men', Charlotte completes a watercolour 'Bess Bell and Mary Gray', and Branwell a watercolour 'Queen Esther'.

1831

7 Jan.	Charlotte completes a crayon drawing of a young lady.
17 Jan.	Charlotte goes to Miss Margaret Wooler's School at Roe Head, Mirfield Moor. The fees are paid for by her godparents, Rev. & Mrs. Thomas Atkinson. She meets Ellen Nussey and Mary Taylor at the school.
25 Jan.	Ellen Nussey arrives at Roe Head.
	Emily and Anne split from Charlotte and Branwell and form their own Kingdom - Gondal.

Jan. / Feb.	Charlotte, at school, draws various facial studies on different days, presumably for an art class.
Mar. / Apr.	Elizabeth Franks (Firth) visits Charlotte at Roe Head.
6 Apr.	Charlotte completes a pencil drawing of a woman.
May	Elizabeth Franks gives Charlotte a dress and muslin and Miss Outhwaite gives her a shawl.
7 May	Branwell completes his 'History of the Young Men'. It is 18 pages long, measures 7.75 x 6.5", has 6 chapters and 15,000 words.
Mid-May	Branwell walks from Haworth to Roe Head and back to visit Charlotte (about 40 miles).
31 May	First letter from Charlotte to Ellen Nussey.
8 June	Branwell writes 'Letters of an Englishman'.
June	Charlotte draws a ruined tower, possibly Guwald Tower, Haddington.
	Branwell starts boxing lessons from John Brown at the Black Bull, Haworth.
July	Charlotte receives three prizes at the end of her first school 'half'.
1 Nov.	Branwell acquires a book of flute music.
14 Dec.	Charlotte wins the French prize at school.
15 Dec.	Charlotte sketches an Irish abbey.

1832

	Charlotte is prepared for confirmation at Mirfield Church by Rev. E. N. Carter (Miss Wooler's brother-in-law).
May	Charlotte leaves Roe Head to teach Emily and Anne at home.

The Rydings, Birstall, home of Ellen Nussey. Branwell declared that he was leaving Charlotte here in 'Paradise'. *(J. Kempson)*

Haworth Sunday School, opened in 1832 at Patrick Brontë's instigation. Charlotte became its first Superintendent. *(J. Kempson)*

24 July	Charlotte draws a portrait of a young lady wearing a garland of flowers.
Sept.	Charlotte's first visit to Ellen Nussey at her home The Rydings, Birstall. She is accompanied by Branwell who declares he is leaving her in 'Paradise'.
10 Oct.	Charlotte completes a wash drawing of Kirkstall Abbey.

During this year the Sunday School near the Parsonage is built at Patrick's instigation and Charlotte becomes the first School Superintendent.

John Brown's new house is built alongside it.

Death of Sir Walter Scott, whose novels had such a profound effect on the Brontës and their writing.

1833

Charlotte writes ' "The Foundling" by Captain Tree', ' "The Green Dwarf" and "Arthuriana" by Lord Charles A. F. Wellesley', and 'The Secret'.

12 Jan.	Charlotte completes a pencil drawing of a seascape.
8 Apr.	Patrick joins Keighley Mechanics Institute. The children frequently use their library.
17 Apr.	Charlotte completes a pencil drawing of Anne.
30 Apr.	Elizabeth Branwell makes her will.
1 July	Branwell sketches a moorland cottage.
6 July	Charlotte completes a watercolour of a landscape with 2 men fishing.
10 July	Ellen Nussey's first visit to Haworth.
21 July	Branwell sketches a hilltop house.
July / Aug.	Emily very ill with erysipelas (inflammation of the skin) on the arm and has to be bled.

14 Aug.	Charlotte completes a watercolour of a French brunette.
Early Sept.	Branwell, Charlotte, Emily and Anne travel by hired gig to meet Ellen Nussey, her brother George and Richard and some friends at the Devonshire Arms Hotel, Bolton Bridge, and visit the abbey ruins.
26 Sept.	M. Heger's first wife and child die in Brussels in a cholera epidemic.
14 Oct.	Charlotte completes a drawing of a young lady.
Autumn	Opening of a new chapel at Woodhouse Grove with the sermon being preached by Rev. Jabez Bunting. It is probable that Patrick and Emily attended.
16 Dec.	Charlotte completes a drawing of boats and a quay.

1834

Feb.	Branwell and Charlotte create their new imaginary Kingdom of Angria.
20 Feb.	Letter from Charlotte to Ellen Nussey referring to the latter's visit to London.
May	Inauguration of the new organ at Haworth church.
June	Patrick takes Charlotte and Branwell to see the Annual Exhibition of the Northern Society for the Encouragement of Fine Arts at Leeds.
17 June	Charlotte paints a water colour of Anne.
4 July	At Ellen Nussey's request, Charlotte sends her a list of recommended reading books.
18 Aug.	A number of clergymen, including Patrick Brontë, make a presentation as a token of respect, to Rev. Hammond Roberson, builder of Liversedge Church, and the inspiration for 'Parson Helstone' in Charlotte's novel 'Shirley'.
23 Aug.	Charlotte does a drawing 'Geneva'.

Anne Brontë, painted by her sister Charlotte in June 1834.

Above: The only known portrait of
Patrick Branwell Brontë.

Right: Emily Brontë — as painted
by Branwell about 1834 and
originally probably part of a group
portrait with her sisters. *(National
Portrait Gallery)*

July/ *Aug.*	Mrs. Gaskell believed that Branwell painted the portrait of his three sisters and, originally, himself, at this time but modern opinion places the painting later.
	Also believed Branwell painted another portrait at this time of his sisters which was later cut up by Mr. Nicholls (Charlotte's husband) and only Emily's likeness kept as it was the only one that was life-like (some believe it was of Anne).
Summer	Painting lessons for all four children being given by William Robinson of Leeds, following the visit in June.
14 Oct.	Charlotte finishes 'My Angria and the Angrians'.
15 Oct.	Charlotte sketches 'An English Lady'.
24 Nov.	Emily and Anne's diary page, written by Emily and signed by both and containing the first reference to Gondal. They have pets called Rainbow, Diamond and Snowflake and a pheasant called Jasper.
26 Dec.	Branwell joins Haworth Temperance Society.

1835

13 Feb.	Death of William Brown, Haworth church sexton and subsequent appointment of his son, John.
End Feb.- *13 Mar.*	Charlotte visits Ellen Nussey at Birstall.
2 Apr.	Death of Rev. John Buckworth (see 1809 and onwards).
End May	Branwell visits Liverpool. Whilst there he buys a copy of Byron's 'Childe Harold's Pilgrimage'.
July	Branwell writes to the Royal Academy of Arts in London concerning possible submission of works.
6 July	Patrick writes to Elizabeth Franks asking her to keep an eye on Charlotte and Emily at Roe Head.
29 July	Charlotte returns to Roe Head as a teacher, with Emily as a pupil.

11 Sept.	Branwell finishes his painting studies with William Robinson.
End Sept./ Early Oct.	Branwell goes to London with references to present himself at the Royal Academy. He never did so, probably drank the money away in a week and returned to Haworth pretending he had been robbed.
Mid Oct.	Emily suffering from severe homesickness, leaves Roe Head.
20 Oct.	Patrick writes his poem 'On Halleys Comet' (published in 1861).
23 Oct.	Emily sketches some cows.
27 Oct.	Anne sketches an oak tree.
13 Nov.	Anne draws an elm tree.
21 Nov.	Death of James Hogg, writer for 'Blackwoods Magazine', to whose editor Branwell subsequently writes offering his services.
7 Dec.	Branwell writes again to the editor of 'Blackwoods Magazine'.
14 Dec.	Charlotte draws 'A Lady's Head'.

1836

Jan.	Anne takes Emily's place at Roe Head.
1 Feb.	Branwell proposed as a Freemason at Haworth Lodge.
10 Feb.	Anne draws a ruined church.
29 Feb.	Branwell initiated as a Freemason.
6 Mar.	Patrick joins the committee of Keighley Mechanics Institute.
22 Mar.	Anne draws a landscape with two men in top hats.
28 Mar.	Branwell passed as a Freemason.

8 Apr.	Branwell again writes to the editor of 'Blackwoods Magazine'.
25 Apr.	Branwell raised as a Freemason.
End May	Charlotte stays with Ellen Nussey.
30 May	Anne draws a house and a landscape.
17-24 June	Charlotte and Anne stay with Mrs. Elizabeth Franks at Huddersfield Vicarage.
21 June	Charlotte and Anne spend the day at Lascelles Hall with Amelia Walker and her family.
23 June	Charlotte draws 'The Cross of Rivaulx'.
Early July	Ellen Nussey visits Charlotte at Haworth.
12 July	It is believed Emily writes her first poem.
July / Aug.	Ellen Nussey moves from Birstall to Brookroyd House, Batley.
11 Aug.	Charlotte writes a description of life at Roe Head.
3 Sept.	Marriage of Monsieur and Madame Heger in Brussels.
19 Sept.	Branwell acts as Secretary at a Masonic meeting.
14 Dec.	Anne is presented with a prize for good conduct at school and she and Charlotte return to Haworth for the holidays.
15 Dec.	Anne draws a landscape.
Dec.	Anne writes her first poem and for the first time the sisters start to date their work and apparently make a serious attempt to collect and assess it.
20 Dec.	Branwell acts as Junior Warden at a Masonic meeting.
29 Dec.	Charlotte first writes to Southey for advice.

Brookroyd House, Batley. Here Charlotte stayed with Ellen Nussey and corrected the proofs of 'Jane Eyre'. *(J. J. Stead)*

Blake Hall, Mirfield, the now demolished house where Anne Brontë became a governess in 1839. *(Chris Sumner collection)*

1837

9 Jan.	Branwell writes for the fourth time to 'Blackwoods Magazine'.
19 Jan.	Branwell writes to Wordsworth seeking advice (no reply).
27 Jan.	Branwell chairs a meeting of the Haworth Operative Conservative Society.
Feb.	Patrick makes a violent verbal attack on the new Poor Law Act at a public meeting in Haworth. (Reported in the Times on 27 Feb.).
Mar.	Southey answers Charlotte's letter of 29 Dec.
16 Mar.	Charlotte writes again to Southey.
22 Mar.	Southey replies to Charlotte's second letter.
20 June	Accession of Princess Victoria to the Throne.
26 June	Emily and Anne's diary paper.
June / July	Branwell acting as Secretary to the Masonic Lodge.
July	Miss Wooler's school moves to Healds House, Dewsbury Moor.
Early Aug.	Charlotte and Anne return to school, now at Dewsbury Moor.
31 Aug.	Anne draws a child's head, one of a set of three.
11 Sept.	Death of Mrs. Elizabeth Franks (Firth).
Autumn	Branwell possibly applies and fails to obtain a post as usher at a school near Halifax, or goes for a few weeks and is dismissed.
15 Nov.	Anne draws a child's head, second of a set of three.
Dec.	Anne, who is unwell, and Charlotte both leave Dewsbury Moor School.

25 Dec.	Branwell is organist at the Masonic Christmas Day service.
Dec. / *Jan.*	Charlotte writes 'Mina Lawry'.

1838

Jan. / *Feb.*	Branwell lodges in Leeds and has lessons in painting from William Robinson at his studio.
	Emily's mastiff 'Keeper' comes to the Parsonage.
8 Mar.	Branwell writes 'The Life of Warner Howard Warner', believed to portray his early childhood memories.
24 Apr.	Emily paints 'Keeper' in watercolours.
May	Branwell sets up a studio as a portrait painter in Bradford. He lodges with a Mr. & Mrs. Kirkby at Fountain Street, and paints their and their niece's portraits.
23 May	Charlotte finally leaves Miss Wooler's school and is presented with a de-luxe edition of Scott's 'The Vision of Don Roderick'.
9 June	Mary and Martha Taylor visit the Parsonage.
28 June	Coronation of Queen Victoria.
31 July	Emily at Bradford copying manuscripts for Branwell.
Autumn	Ellen Nussey, who has been in London and Bath with her brother, visits the Parsonage for the first time in two years.
Sept.	Emily goes to Law Hill, Southowram, Halifax, as a teacher, specialising in music. The owner is a Miss Patchett. Much of the inspiration for 'Wuthering Heights' springs from this time.
2 Oct.	Charlotte writes to Ellen Nussey referring to the hardship Emily is suffering at Law Hill, (probable date - letter is dated 1836 but postmarked 1838).

Dec.	Charlotte visits Ellen Nussey at Brookroyd.
22 Dec.	Branwell paints Thomas Parker of Haworth.

1839

10 Jan.	Patrick writes to Rev. Franks for help in finding a clerical assistant.
21 Jan.	Charlotte visits the Walkers at Lascelles Hall.
28 Feb.	Charlotte receives a proposal of marriage from Henry Nussey, Ellen's brother.
Feb. / Mar.	Martha and Mary Taylor visit Haworth.
5 Mar.	Charlotte writes to Henry Nussey refusing his proposal.
12 Mar.	Charlotte writes to Ellen Nussey to tell her of her brother's proposal and the reasons for her refusal.
Mar. / Apr.	Probable date when Emily leaves Law Hill.
8 Apr.	Anne becomes governess at Mrs. Ingham's, Blake Hall, Mirfield. She attends Mirfield Church and visits the Moravian settlement.
May	Charlotte becomes governess at Mrs. Sidgwick's, Stonegappe, near Skipton. She becomes friendly with the Rev. E. M. Carter and his family.
24 May	Charlotte completes a pencil drawing of a Roman ruin.
Mid-May	Branwell gives up his studio at Bradford and returns to Haworth.
30 May	Patrick nominates William Weightman as curate at Haworth.
June	Patrick and Branwell agree to study various Greek classics.

c14 June- *c19 July*	Charlotte goes with her employers to stay with their relatives, the Greenwoods, at 'Swarcliffe', Birstwith, near Harrogate, after which she leaves her employment.
July	Branwell visits Liverpool.
	Charlotte and Ellen Nussey discuss the possibility of a holiday together at Cleathorpe (Cleethorpes).
Aug.	Charlotte receives a proposal of marriage from Rev. David Bryce.
	Arrival of Rev. William Weightman M.A. as curate at Haworth.
	Branwell visits Liverpool.
Mid- *Sept.*	Charlotte and Ellen Nussey go on holiday to Easton House, near Burlington (Bridlington) and she has her first view of the sea. Whilst there she does a watercolour of Easton House. She and Ellen Nussey also spend some time in lodgings near the harbour in Burlington.
Autumn	About this time Branwell, depressed about his failure at Bradford, reads Thomas de Quincey's 'Confessions of an English Opium Eater' and himself starts taking opium.
13 Nov.	Anne sketches a girl looking out to sea.
Dec.	Anne leaves her employment at Blake Hall, Mirfield.
21 Dec.	Tabby falls in Kirkgate and breaks her leg. She leaves the Parsonage to stay with her sister in Stubbing Lane. John Brown, the sexton, sends his oldest daughter to help out at the Parsonage. Tabby later returns and is looked after by the children.
31 Dec.	Branwell goes as tutor to the family of Mr. Postlethwaite at Broughton House, Broughton in Furness, Ulverston.

Haworth Main Street in 1928 — long before the days of souvenir shops.

1840

17 Jan.	Death of Rev. David Bryce (see 1839).
Feb. / *Mar.*	Ellen Nussey stays at the Parsonage for 3 weeks. She nicknames Emily 'The Major' for protecting her from the amorous advances of William Weightman, the curate.
14 Feb.	All three sisters and Ellen Nussey receive a valentine card from William Weightman. All the girls are fond of him, but Anne probably falls in love with him.
2 Mar.	Branwell draws Broughton Church.
Mar.	William Morgan visits Patrick.
Apr.	Patrick lectures at Keighley Mechanics Institute.
15 Apr.	Branwell sends copies of his poem 'Sir Henry Tunstall' to Blackwoods Magazine and to Thomas de Quincey.
20 Apr.	Branwell sends a specimen translation of Horace's Odes to Hartley Coleridge.
1 May	Branwell visits Hartley Coleridge at Ambleside.
1 June	Branwell is dismissed from his position at Broughton in Furness.
June	Mary Taylor visits Haworth.
27 June	Branwell writes again to Hartley Coleridge.
July	Charlotte writes for advice to Wordsworth.
14 July	William Weightman leaves for his ordination at Ripon.
13 / 14 *Aug.*	Visit to Haworth of Mrs. Maria Brontë's cousin, John Branwell Williams, his wife and daughter Eliza.
31 Aug.	Branwell appointed Assistant Clerk-in-charge at Sowerby Bridge Railway Station at £75 p.a.

Sept.	William Weightman returns.
	Charlotte writes for a position as teacher with a Mrs. Brooke of Huddersfield.
	Branwell commences work at Sowerby Bridge.
5 Oct.	Sowerby Bridge Railway Station and its line is opened.

1841

11 Jan.	Charlotte writes to Henry Nussey on the subject of Ellen's possible marriage to a Mr. Vincent.
Feb.	Patrick trying to obtain apprenticeships for local orphans.
Mar.	Mary Taylor announces her intention of emigrating to New Zealand.
	Anne goes as governess to Mrs. Robinson at Thorp Green Hall, Little Ouseburn, near York.
2 Mar.	Charlotte goes as a governess to Mrs. White of Upperwood House, Rawdon.
Apr.	Martha Taylor goes to school in Brussels.
1 Apr.	Branwell is transferred to Luddendon Foot Railway Station near Halifax as Clerk in Charge at £130 p.a.
25 Apr.	Charlotte goes to Ellen Nussey's for the day.
June	The family cat 'Black Tom' dies. Other family pets at the time are two geese 'Victoria' and 'Adelaide', a canary, 'Little Duck' and a hawk 'Hero'.
June	Anne home for a holiday.
30 June	Charlotte home for about two or three weeks.
July	Charlotte, Emily and Anne discuss the possibility of setting up a school with financial assistance from Aunt Branwell.

Mid July	Anne returns to work and goes to Scarborough with her employers.
30 July	Emily and Anne write their diary papers. Emily at Haworth and Anne at Scarborough.
July / *Aug.*	Charlotte receives a dramatic letter from Mary Taylor describing Brussels. Mary Taylor had just joined her sister in Brussels.
Aug.	Branwell becomes the first of the Brontë children in print with a poem in the Halifax Guardian.
7 Aug.	Charlotte writes of having received a black silk scarf and kid gloves from Mary Taylor in Brussels.
9 Aug.	Death of Rev. Hammond Roberson.
Aug. / *Sept.*	Miss Wooler offers to sell her school at Dewsbury Moor to Charlotte.
Sept.	Charlotte's employers, Mr. & Mrs. White, suggest she go abroad to study before setting up her own school.
29 Sept.	Charlotte asks for financial help in going to school in Brussels, from Aunt Branwell.
6 Oct.	Emily sketches a curly haired girl.
13 Oct.	Death of Rev. John Fennell. He is buried at Cross Stone Church, near Todmorden.
17 Oct.	Charlotte declines Miss Wooler's offer of her school.
c25 Oct.	Branwell attends a performance of 'The Creation' at Halifax.
27 Oct.	Emily draws her pet merlin hawk 'Hero'.
10, 19 & *29 Nov.*	Patrick writes to the Ordnance Office offering advice on alterations to the musket in use in the British Army. He had a life-long interest and some expertise in firearms.
10 Dec.	Charlotte writes to Hartley Coleridge and sends him a copy of her first attempt at a novel 'Ashworth'.

24 Dec.	Charlotte leaves the Whites at Rawdon.
25 Dec.	Ann home for the holidays and she and Emily begin their prose writings of the Gondal Chronicles.

1842

Jan.	Anne is persuaded by the Robinsons to stay at Thorp Green despite her wish to leave.
20 Jan.	Charlotte refers to William Weightman flirting with Anne.
1 Feb.	Charlotte gives Emily a prayerbook.
2 Feb.	Ordnance Office rejects Patrick's suggestion of Nov. 1841.
8 Feb. (Tues.)	Charlotte and Emily with Mr. Brontë and Mary and Joe Taylor go to London en route to Brussels. They leave Leeds Railway Station at 9 a.m. and arrive London at 8 p.m.
12 Feb. (Sat.)	They leave London for Ostend.
14 Feb. (Mon.)	They travel from Ostend to Brussels and stay at the Hotel de Hollande.
15 Feb. (Tues.)	Charlotte and Emily present themselves at their new school Pensionnat Heger, together with the British Chaplain Mr. Jenkins and Mrs. Jenkins.
	Patrick spends another week travelling in Belgium and France before returning to Haworth.
26 Mar.	Charlotte and Emily spend the day with Mary and Martha Taylor at Koekelberg.
28 Mar.	Mdme. Heger gives birth to a son, Prospere.
31 Mar.	Branwell is dismissed from the railway.
4 Apr.	Confirmation of Branwell's dismissal at a directors' meeting held at Hunts Bank, Manchester.

11 Apr.	The directors reject an appeal by local patrons against Branwell's dismissal.
3 May	Death of Haworth's surgeon, Thomas Andrew. A monument is later erected to him and at Branwell's instigation, his friend Joseph Leyland receives the commission.
7 & 14 May	Branwell has poems printed in the Halifax Guardian.
20 May	Joseph Leyland visits Haworth and dines at the Parsonage.
May	Arrival of the Wheelwrights at Brussels.
Whitsun	Charlotte and Emily spend the holiday with Mary and Martha Taylor who are at school just outside Brussels.
24 June	Anne draws a lady.
31 July	Charlotte writes her French essay 'Portrait de Pierre L'Hermite' and Emily 'Portrait de Harold' (King Harold I of England).
Aug.	Charlotte gives a sketch to Madame Heger as a 'token of affection and respect'.
12 Aug.	School party at Pensionnat Heger.
15 Aug.	The school closes for the summer. Charlotte and Emily remain with the five Wheelwright girls (their parents were in Germany), two other foreign girls and a skeleton staff of servants.
6 Sept. (Tues.)	William Weightman dies at Haworth of cholera. Branwell, who has helped to nurse him, is profoundly affected by his death.
10 Sept.	William Weightman's funeral, conducted by Patrick.
Sept.	Branwell writes a fourth time to Blackwoods Magazine.
2 Oct.	Patrick delivers William Weightman's funeral sermon.
12 Oct.	Martha Taylor dies of cholera in Brussels.

13 Oct.	Charlotte goes to Koekelberg to see Martha, but too late.
14 Oct.	Martha Taylor's funeral at the Chapel Royal.
29 Oct. (Sat.)	Elizabeth Branwell dies at Haworth.
30 Oct.	Charlotte and Emily visit Mary Taylor and go with her to Martha's grave at the Protestant cemetery in Brussels.
2 Nov. (Wed.)	Charlotte and Emily receive news of Aunt Branwell's illness and plan to return home.
3 Nov.	Elizabeth Branwell's funeral conducted by Rev. James Bradley of Oakworth.
5 Nov.	Charlotte and Emily leave Brussels for home and as they do, hear of Aunt Branwell's death.
6 Nov.	Charlotte and Emily catch the steamer at Antwerp.
8 Nov.	Charlotte and Emily arrive back at Haworth.
29 Nov.	Anne returns to Thorp Green.
29 Nov.- 5 Dec.	Charlotte stays with Ellen Nussey at Brookroyd.
25 Dec.	Anne home for the holidays.
26 Dec.	Branwell attends his last Masonic meeting.
28 Dec.	Elizabeth Branwell's will proved. £1500 is divided equally between Charlotte, Emily, Anne and their cousin in Penzance, Elizabeth Kingston.
Late Dec.	Tabby returns to the Parsonage. Martha Brown, John Brown's daughter, comes as servant.

1843

Jan.	Ellen Nussey visits Haworth.
	Anne returns to Thorp Green with Branwell accompanying her as tutor.

Charlotte Brontë — from a chalk drawing by George Richmond, R.A.
(National Portrait Gallery)

15 Jan.	In a letter to Ellen Nussey, Charlotte refers to her marrying Joe Taylor.
27 Jan.	Charlotte returns to Brussels, leaving Emily at home. She now combines teaching and learning.
28 Jan.	Charlotte arrives in Brussels.
30 Jan.	Mary Dixon calls on Charlotte in Brussels. She forms a friendship with the Dixon family, who live there.
1 Mar.	Charlotte visits the Carnival held prior to the Lent fast with M. Heger and one of the pupils.
Apr. / May	Patrick visits Anne and Branwell at Thorp Green.
24 Apr.	Anne buys a copy of 'Sacred Harmony'.
1 May	M. Heger gives Charlotte a little German Testament.
May	Charlotte is planning a novel and notes down its plot inside the front cover of her exercise book. The plot is similar to 'Villette'.
29 May	Charlotte writes home for more money.
31 May	Charlotte writes 'Sur La Mort de Napoleon'.
June	Anne buys a music manuscript book.
	Anne returns to Haworth for the holidays, bringing Flossie with her.
16 June	Death of Sarah Walker Nussey (Ellen's sister).
6 Aug.	Charlotte writes to Ellen Nussey complaining of the loneliness and her desire to come home.
15 Aug.	M. Heger gives Charlotte a two volume edition of the works of Bernadin St. Pierre as the Hegers leave for their holidays.
	Charlotte attends a 10 p.m. concert in the park. This day is a public holiday marking the Assumption of the Virgin.
24 Aug.	Anne buys a sketching block.

1 Sept.	Charlotte visits the Protestant cemetery in Brussels and then, very lonely and unhappy, attends confession at the Catholic Cathedral of St. Gudule.
10 Sept.	Charlotte sees Queen Victoria in Brussels.
14 Sept.	Anne buys a German dictionary.
Oct.	Charlotte hands in her notice but is persuaded to stay by M. Heger.
19 Oct.	Anne, at Thorp Green, draws a man and a dog.
Nov.	Anne buys Valpy's 'Delectus' in Latin.
15 Nov.	Mdme. Heger gives birth to a daughter, Julie, her fifth child.
20 Nov.	Patrick writes to his brother Hugh, at Ballynaskeagh asking how things are with the Protestant/Catholic troubles in Ireland.
10 Dec.	Charlotte attends a concert at the Salle de la Grande Harmonie, also attended by the King and Queen of the Belgians.
16 Dec.	Anne draws a country scene.
17 Dec.	Charlotte finally decides to return home and is given a parting gift of a little box by Mlle Sophie - a fellow teacher.
19 Dec.	Charlotte writes to tell Emily she is returning.
25 Dec.	Charlotte spends Christmas with Mr. & Mrs. Jenkins.
Christmas	Anne and Emily probably discussed and reorganised their poetry over the holiday.
29 Dec.	M. Heger presents Charlotte with a diploma.

1844

1 Jan.	Charlotte, accompanied by Mdme Heger, leaves Brussels for Ostend. M. Heger gives her an anthology of French poetry.

2 Jan.	Charlotte sails from Ostend to return home.
3 Jan.	Charlotte arrives back in Haworth.
Jan.	Emily begins to copy out her poems and classify them as Gondal or non-Gondal.
	Anne buys a copy of Hannah Moore's 'Sketches and Opinions'.
	Patrick's eyesight worsening.
Mid-Jan.	Ellen Nussey stays with Charlotte at Haworth and is given one of Flossie's puppies.
20 Jan.	Anne and Branwell rejoin the Robinsons at York.
Mar.	The cat 'Tiger' dies.
7 Mar.	Anne buys a copy of 'Deutches Leserbuch'.
7-24 Mar.	Charlotte visits Ellen Nussey.
16 Mar.	Patrick writes to the 'Leeds Mercury' about fire precautions in the home.
Apr.	Charlotte probably tells Emily of her love for M. Heger.
May	Charlotte stays a few days with Mary Taylor.
c20 June	Branwell and Anne return to Haworth from Thorp Green. Branwell is 'irritable'.
June/ July	Ellen Nussey visits Haworth where great attention is paid to her by Patrick's curate, Rev. James William Smith.
July	Charlotte is offered a position as a teacher at a Manchester School at a salary of £100 p.a., but declines.
July- Oct.	Charlotte and Emily and (to a lesser extent) Anne attempt to start up a school at the Parsonage.
21 July	Rev. Samuel Redhead (see 1819) preaches at Haworth and is given a good welcome.

24 July	Charlotte writes to M. Heger telling him of her school plans and her need to see him again.
29 July	Charlotte sends some prospecti of the planned school to Ellen Nussey to circulate amongst her acquaintances.
Aug.	Rev. Smith, the curate, leaves Haworth for Keighley and is replaced by the Rev. Joseph Brett Grant.
25 Aug.	Branwell, at Thorp Green, does an ink drawing of some rural buildings.
Sept.	Mary Taylor tells Charlotte that she is emigrating to New Zealand.
2 Oct.	Charlotte writes and thanks Ellen Nussey for her attempts to get pupils for the school and says they have now dropped the plan.
24 Oct.	Charlotte sends another letter to M. Heger, via Joe Taylor who is going to Brussels. All her letters are ignored.
Nov.	Anne buys sets of piano music.
14 Nov.	Ellen Nussey tells Charlotte of her brother Henry's prospective marriage and appointment to Hathersage in Derbyshire.
Dec.	Anne and Branwell come home for Christmas and Charlotte declines an invitation from Ellen Nussey for Anne and herself to spend Christmas with her at Brookroyd.
Christmas	Anne writes 'Lines inscribed on a dungeon wall'.

1845

Jan.	George Nussey, Ellen's brother, seriously ill.
4 Jan.	Mary Taylor visits Charlotte at Haworth.
8 Jan.	Charlotte writes to M. Heger, not having heard from him since April 1844.
18 Jan.	Anne and Branwell return to Thorp Green.

Feb.	Charlotte visits Mary Taylor at Hunsworth House to say goodbye before she goes to New Zealand. They are joined by Ellen Nussey.
Mar.	Mary Taylor emigrates with her brother, Waring, to New Zealand.
29 Apr.	Meeting at Haworth Church between Patrick and Joseph Rushworth of Mouldgreave to discuss new bells for the church.
18 May	Charlotte writes again to M. Heger.
22 May	Marriage of Henry Nussey to Miss Emily Prescott.
25 May	Rev. Arthur Bell Nicholls comes to Haworth as curate.
9 June	Rev. Nicholls is licensed to the curacy of Haworth.
11 June	Anne and Branwell leave Thorp Green - Anne for good, Branwell for holidays.
c18 June	Branwell returns alone to Thorp Green.
30 June- *2 July*	Emily and Anne spend some time at York, sleeping at York one night and Keighley the next.
3 July	Charlotte goes to Hathersage with Ellen Nussey to prepare the vicarage for her newly-wedded brother, Henry. Here she would have seen the Eyre brasses in the church. ·
4 July	The Robinsons leave Thorp Green for their annual holidays at Scarborough, leaving Branwell with their son, Edmund.
17 July	Edmund Robinson joins his parents. Branwell returns to Haworth where he subsequently (probably 21st) receives a letter of dismissal from Mr. Robinson for his 'proceedings . . . bad beyond expression.' Branwell alleges that he and Mrs. Robinson were in love, but the whole affair is a mystery. Branwell's grief is totally without any self-control. The family accept his explanation.
26 July	Charlotte arrives back at Haworth from Hathersage at

Hathersage Vicarage in Derbyshire, where Charlotte stayed with Ellen Nussey in 1845, to prepare it for Ellen's brother, the Rev. Henry Nussey. The new incumbent was then on his honeymoon, have previously proposed marriage to Charlotte. *(J. Kempson)*

Haworth Parsonage from the churchyard — a recent view. *(A. K. McCluskey)*

10 p.m. to find Branwell ill, as a result of his dismissal. He is virtually beyond the control of his family.

29 July-
3 Aug.
Branwell goes with John Brown, the sexton, to Liverpool and North Wales to recover from the shock of his dismissal.

31 July
Anne and Emily's diary papers, opened a day late. Charlotte writes to tell Ellen Nussey about Branwell.

26 Aug.
Death of Rev. Samuel Redhead (see 1819).

10 Sept.
Branwell writes to his friend, J. B. Leyland, and indicates that he has written a 3 volume novel. It was later suggested this was 'Wuthering Heights'.

Oct.
Branwell writes to Francis Grundy and explains his version of the Thorp Green affair.

c9 Oct.
Charlotte finds the poems written by Emily. She is subsequently shown poems by Anne and, largely against Emily's wishes, they publish at their own expense a collection of their poems under the nom-de-plumes Currer, Ellis and Acton Bell. Emily insists on anonymity. The name 'Bell' may have come from Rev. Arthur Bell Nicholls, and 'Currer' from Miss Frances Mary Richardson Currer.

20 Oct.
The Robinson's eldest daughter Lydia elopes with Henry Roxton, leading actor from the Theatre Royal, Scarborough, and is cut out of her father's will.

23 Oct.
Branwell writes an application for a position as Secretary to the Manchester, Hebden Bridge and Carlisle Junction Railway.

Autumn /
Winter
During this time Emily is writing 'Wuthering Heights', Anne 'Agnes Grey' and Charlotte 'The Professor'.

18 Nov.
Charlotte writes to M. Heger for the last time.

25 Nov.
Branwell sends his poem 'Penmaenmawr' (written whilst in Wales with John Brown) to Leyland and asks him to insert it in the Halifax Guardian.

Christmas	Ellen Nussey sends slippers to Charlotte.

1846

Jan.- *June*	The three sisters still writing their first novels.
Jan.	Fall in the price of railway shares causes the sisters some worries as they have money invested.
28 Jan.	Charlotte writes to the publishers Aylott and Jones to see if they will publish their poems.
6 Feb.	Charlotte sends the manuscript of the poems to Aylott and Jones.
5-21 Feb.	Charlotte corresponding with publishers over paper and printing costs.
c18 Feb.- *2 Mar.*	Charlotte visits Ellen Nussey at Brookroyd.
Mar.	Branwell deteriorating.
3 Mar.	Charlotte sends the cost of publishing the poems (£31.10.0) to Aylott and Jones.
10 Mar.	New bells hung in Haworth Church (see April 1845).
11 Mar.	Aylott and Jones send the proofs of the poem collection to Charlotte.
6 Apr.	Charlotte writes to Aylott and Jones to say that they have 3 novels in preparation.
Apr.	Branwell goes to Halifax for 3 days.
20 Apr.	Charlotte asks for 3 copies of the poems and inquires about advertising.
28 Apr.	Branwell writes to J. B. Leyland saying he has material for a novel.
11 May	Anne writes a poem which suggests Emily is still furious over Charlotte's reading her poems in October

1845. Charlotte instructs Aylott & Jones to spend more than £2 on advertising.

c21 May Publication of 'Poems by Currer, Ellis and Acton Bell'.

25 May Charlotte sends a further £5 for expenses to Aylott & Jones.

26 May Death of Rev. Edmund Robinson of Thorp Green, Anne and Branwell's former employer.

1/2 June George Gooch, the Robinson's coachman, comes to see Branwell at Haworth. Branwell explains that he expects it to be to tell him to go to Mrs. Robinson but it is to say she cannot see him, or she will be removed from the will. This provision was not in the will and we only have Branwell's version of what Gooch wanted.

17 June Charlotte writes to tell Ellen Nussey about the Robinsons and says that Branwell has 'given up'.

27 June Charlotte completes her fair copy of 'The Professor'.

July George Gooch again visits Haworth and Branwell says that it is to tell him that Mrs. Robinson is declining in health.

4 July Edition of the 'Athenaeum' giving a review of the poems.

Charlotte writes to the publisher, Henry Colburn, sending the manuscripts of 'The Professor', 'Wuthering Heights' and 'Agnes Grey'.

14 July Mrs. Robinson and her children go on their annual holidays - Whitby (3 days), Hartlepool (3 days) and Redcar (3 weeks).

Mid July-Aug. Charlotte suffering badly from toothache.

End July/Aug. Charlotte takes her father to Manchester to see a consultant about his worsening eyesight.

19 Aug. Charlotte accompanies Patrick to Manchester for a cataract operation by Dr. William Wilson (on 25 August). They take lodgings at 83 Mount Pleasant,

	Boundary Street, Oxford Road, Manchester, and while her father is recuperating from the operation, Charlotte starts writing 'Jane Eyre'.
20 Sept.	Rev. A. B. Nicholls ordained priest by the Bishop of Ripon.
28 Sept.	Charlotte and Patrick return to Haworth from Manchester.
6 Oct.	Charlotte writes to the editor of the Dublin University Magazine to thank him for his favourable review of the poems.
Nov.	Rev. Nicholls returns to Ireland for a holiday.
17 Nov.	Patrick resumes his full pastoral duties following his operation.
Early Dec.	Anne suffering badly from asthma.
6 Dec.	A sheriff's officer visits Branwell and threatens him with prison if he doesn't pay his debts.
Dec.-Feb.	Very cold winter. All the family suffer from colds.
	Mrs. Robinson's doctor, Dr. Crosby visits Haworth on several occasions, allegedly to bring money to Branwell.

1847

Jan.	Charlotte receives a letter from Ellen Nussey, apparently opened in transit, containing a present of some cuffs.
Jan./Feb.	Anne receiving frequent letters from her former pupils, the daughters of Mrs. Robinson.
1 Mar.	Charlotte writes to Ellen Nussey and tells her that the Misses Robinson, Elizabeth and Mary, have written to Anne every day for a fortnight.
Apr.	Whole family ill with colds.
3 Apr.	Charlotte visited at Haworth by the wife of a former

	Haworth curate, Mrs. Collins and her daughter, who she had previously met in Manchester, Mrs. Collins having been abandoned by her husband.
21 Apr.	Charlotte forgets her own birthday and Ellen Nussey's on the 22nd.
May	Ellen Nussey breaks arrangements to visit Haworth, leading to angry letters from Charlotte.
16 June	Charlotte sends unsold copies of the Poems to De Quincey, Hartley Coleridge, Lockhart, Wordsworth and Tennyson.
Early July	The Publisher T. C. Newby accepts 'Wuthering Heights' and 'Agnes Grey' but declines 'The Professor'.
15 July	Charlotte sends 'The Professor' to Smith, Elder & Company.
Mid-July	J. B. Leyland visits Branwell at Haworth.
July / Aug.	Ellen Nussey stays with Charlotte at Haworth.
2 Aug.	As she has heard nothing, Charlotte writes again to Smith, Elder & Company.
6 Aug.	Charlotte receives a letter from Smith, Elder & Company rejecting 'The Professor' but indicating that another novel might be acceptable.
24 Aug.	Charlotte sends 'Jane Eyre' to Smith, Elder & Company, which is instantly accepted.
Sept.	Charlotte goes to stay with Ellen Nussey, and there, clandestinely, corrects the proofs of 'Jane Eyre'.
	The Parsonage well is cleared out for the first time in 20 years. Eight rusty tins are found in it!
Oct.	Branwell getting even more difficult.
7-15 Oct.	Rev. Nicholls away from Haworth. Charlotte refers to his being narrow-minded.

The ruins of Wycoller Hall — the Ferndean Manor of 'Jane Eyre'. *(Chris Sumner)*

Red House, Gomersal — home of Charlotte's friend Mary Taylor and her family, on which the Yorke family in 'Shirley' were based. *(J. Kempson)*

16 Oct.	'Jane Eyre' is published, under the nom-de-plume Currer Bell, and is a huge success.
19 Oct.	Charlotte receives six complimentary copies of 'Jane Eyre' from the publishers.
23 Oct.	Having been sent a complimentary copy, Thackeray writes to Smith, Elder & Company to praise 'Jane Eyre' which he read at one sitting.
Nov.	Anne starts writing her biographical poem 'Self-Communion'.
Nov. / Dec.	Charlotte attempts to re-write 'The Professor' variously titled 'John Henry' and 'The Moores'
Early Dec.	'Wuthering Heights' and 'Agnes Grey' published under the nom-de-plumes of Ellis and Acton Bell respectively. The publisher tries to cash in on 'Jane Eyre's' popularity and pretends they are by the same author. Charlotte starts work on a new novel.
10 Dec.	Charlotte receives her first payment for 'Jane Eyre' - £100?
c14 Dec.	Emily and Anne receive six copies of 'Wuthering Heights' and 'Agnes Grey' from the publishers and find them full of errors.
21 Dec.	Charlotte writes her preface to the second edition of 'Jane Eyre' and dedicates it to her literary idol Thackeray, which is unfortunate as unbeknown to Charlotte, he has a mad wife.

1848

Jan.	Second edition of 'Jane Eyre' published. Branwell visits Halifax. He is now having occasional fits. The publisher, T. C. Newby, is attempting to pass off 'Wuthering Heights' and 'Agnes Grey' as written by Charlotte.

15 Feb.	Letter from Newby to Emily referring to her second novel and its publication.
17 Feb.	Charlotte receives a further £100 for 'Jane Eyre'.
Mar.	All three sisters ill with 'flu.
Apr.	Third edition of 'Jane Eyre' published.
20 Apr.	Charlotte receives the first of many parcels of complimentary books from Smith, Elder & Company.
3 May	In a letter to Ellen Nussey, Charlotte denies she is the author of 'Jane Eyre'.
June	Anne sends 'The Tenant of Wildfell Hall' to her publishers.
	Branwell is threatened with arrest for debt.
	Ellen Nussey again suggests Charlotte has written 'Jane Eyre'.
July	Branwell now sleeping all day and awake all night. He is sharing Patrick's room so that someone is with him.
	The Parsonage is painted externally by John Hudson for 18/-.
Early July	'The Tenant of Wildfell Hall' is published.
4 July	Patrick writes to the Ordnance Department with plans of a mortar he has designed.
7 July (Fri.)	Charlotte and Anne go to London to see Smith, Elder & Co. and assure them that they are three distinct people and to see T. C. Newby.
8 July (Sat.)	Charlotte and Anne introduce themselves to George Smith of Smith, Elder & Company. In the evening they go with George Smith and his sisters Eliza and Sarah to see Rossini's 'Barber of Seville' at Covent Garden.
9 July (Sun.)	Charlotte and Anne go with Mr. Williams (Smith's reader who discovered 'Jane Eyre') to hear Dr. Croly, Rector of St. Stephens, Walbrook, but he was not

preaching. They then go to dinner with Mr. Smith at his home - 4 Westbourne Place, Paddington.

10 July (Mon.)	Charlotte and Anne take tea at Mr. Williams' house. They also visit the Royal Academy, the National Gallery and dine again at Mr. Smith's house. They buy Tennyson's poems 'The Princess' for Emily and a book each for Tabby and Martha.
11 July	Charlotte and Anne leave London for Haworth, arriving home on 12 July.
22 July	Patrick receives a letter from Thomas Watson Nicholson, landlord of the 'Old Cock' Inn, Halifax, threatening a summons if Branwell's debts are not paid.
4 Aug.	Death of Lady Scott (see 8 Nov.), wife of Sir Edward Dolman Scott.
22 Aug.	Ordnance Department reply to Patrick saying that the mortar design he suggested is already in use.
22 Sept.	Branwell visits John Brown's house in Parsonage Lane. His last visit into the village.
22 Sept. (evening)	Francis Grundy visits Haworth and by arrangement with Patrick meets Branwell in the 'Black Bull'. Branwell is apparently mentally disturbed.
24 Sept. (Sun.)	Branwell dies shortly after 9 a.m.
28 Sept.	Branwell's funeral, conducted by William Morgan.
28/29 Sept.	Charlotte unwell.
30 Sept.	Report of Branwell's death in the Leeds Mercury.
1 Oct.	Branwell's funeral sermon in Haworth Church, preached by Rev. Nicholls. Also the last time Emily leaves the house.
9 Oct.	Charlotte ill with headaches and sickness and Emily ill with cough and cold.

Mid-Oct.	Emily seriously ill with shortage of breath, but refuses to see a doctor.
18 Oct.	Charlotte so ill she is unable to write.
19 Oct.	Anne's former pupil, Mary Robinson, marries Henry Clapham at Allstree and goes to live at Ayreworth House, Keighley.
25 Oct.	Publication of Mrs. Gaskell's first book 'Mary Barton'.
29 Oct.	Charlotte writes to Ellen Nussey expressing concern at Emily's health.
7 Nov.	Emily too ill to write.
8 Nov.	Mrs. Robinson marries Sir Edward Dolman Scott (see 4 August).
23 Nov.	Emily very ill but still refusing to see a doctor.
c3 Dec.	The two Robinson sisters visit Anne at Haworth.
9 Dec.	Charlotte writes to a Dr. Epps giving details of Emily's symptoms.
18 Dec. (Mon.)	Emily collapses at the kitchen door when trying to feed the dogs but still refuses all medical help.
19 Dec. (Tues.)	Emily says that she will see a doctor but before one can come, she dies at 2 p.m.
22 Dec.	Emily's funeral conducted by Rev. A. B. Nicholls.
Late-Dec.	Both Patrick and Anne ill with influenza.
	Ellen Nussey comes to Haworth following Charlotte's plea for her to come.

1849

5 Jan.	Anne is visited by Mr. Thomas Pridgin Teale, surgeon to Leeds General Infirmary, who diagnoses her illness as fatal.

10 Jan.	Anne being treated with blisters and cod liver oil.
	Charlotte writes to Ellen Nussey expressing her fears about Anne's health. She encloses a copy of 'Wuthering Heights' thus admitting their authorships.
15 Jan.	Charlotte is unwell.
Mid-Jan.	Patrick now recovered from the flu.
28 Jan.	Anne completes her last poem.
End-Jan.	Charlotte sends the first volume of 'Shirley' to the publishers.
5 Feb.	Administration of Emily's estate - she died intestate with a sum under £450.
14 Feb.	Death of Anne's godmother, Fanny Outhwaite.
5 Apr.	Anne writes to Ellen Nussey, declining her invitation to stay at Brookroyd, but suggesting she may accompany Charlotte and herself to the seaside.
Spring / Summer	Bad sanitation and lack of fresh water cause many deaths in Haworth
Early May	Anne is left £200 in Miss Outhwaite's will.
23 May	Intention of Charlotte to take Anne to Scarborough via Leeds, where they will meet Ellen Nussey, and York, where they will visit the Minster, but Anne too ill.
24 May	Since no word of Anne's inability to travel could be sent to stop Ellen Nussey going to Leeds to meet them, she comes to Haworth and the three travel to York and stay at the George Hotel.
25 May	The three arrive at Scarborough.
26 May	They take a ride onto the sands and Anne drives the donkey and cart on a ride herself to avoid any unnecessary cruelty by the handler.

28 May (Mon.)	Anne dies at their lodgings at 2 p.m.
29 May	Charlotte writes to her father to tell him of Anne's death and that she will be buried at Scarborough.
30 May	Patrick receives Charlotte's letter.
	Funeral of Anne at St. Mary's Church, Scarborough.
	Charlotte and Ellen Nussey stay on at Scarborough.
7 June	Charlotte and Ellen Nussey leave Scarborough and go to Cliff House, Filey.
14 June	Charlotte and Ellen Nussey leave Filey and stay with the Hudsons at Easton, near Bridlington. Charlotte continues writing 'Shirley'.
21 June (Thurs.)	Charlotte arrives home just before 8 p.m.
27 July	Charlotte sends £4.10s. to Ellen Nussey to get her a bath shower, a fur boa and some cuffs.
Aug.	Patrick has a severe attack of bronchitis.
8 Aug.	A petition for sanitary and water improvements in Haworth is sent to the General Board of Health in London.
28 Aug.	Charlotte finishes 'Shirley'.
Sept.	Both Tabby and Martha Brown ill in bed at the Parsonage. Tabitha Brown and her mother help out.
6 Sept.	Administration of Anne's estate - she died intestate with a sum under £600.
8 Sept. (Sat.)	James Taylor of Smith, Elder & Company comes to Haworth to collect the 'Shirley' manuscript.
10 Sept.	Charlotte ill with a bilious attack.
c28 Sept.	The bath shower arrives (see 27 July).

Shibden Hall, Halifax, often thought to be the Thrushcross Grange of 'Wuthering Heights'. *(J. Kempson)*

Top Withens, before it became a restored ruin. It is thought by some to be 'Wuthering Heights', which in reality is much more likely to have been modelled on High Sunderland Hall, near Halifax.

Oct.	Charlotte concerned about the fall in value of her railway shares.
24-31 Oct.	Charlotte stays with Ellen Nussey.
26 Oct.	'Shirley' published.
Nov.	Article in a Liverpool paper suggesting that Currer Bell might be Charlotte Brontë.
5 Nov.	Charlotte receives her complimentary copies of 'Shirley'.
20 Nov.	Charlotte receives her first letter from Mrs. Gaskell and she sends a copy of 'Shirley' to Harriet Martineau.
29 Nov. (Thurs.)	Charlotte goes to stay with the Smiths in London.
3 Dec. (Mon.)	Charlotte meets Thackeray at a dinner at the Smith's house.
9 Dec. (Sun.)	Charlotte has tea with Harriet Martineau and finally reveals herself to be Currer Bell.
c12 Dec.	Charlotte leaves the Smiths and spends two days with the Wheelwrights at Kensington.
14 Dec.	Charlotte dines with the literary critics of 'The Times', 'Athenaeum', 'Spectator', 'Examiner' and 'Atlas'.
15 Dec.	Charlotte returns to Haworth.
18 Dec.	Patrick writes a hymn for the Sunday School.
21 Dec.	Joe Taylor (Mary's brother) visits the Parsonage for dinner and invites Charlotte to spend Christmas with the Taylors and their cousins, the Dixons, at Hay Hall, Birmingham. Charlotte declines.
28 Dec.	Ellen Nussey comes to stay at the Parsonage.

1850

Jan.	Now widely known that Charlotte is Currer Bell and the first tourists start to visit Haworth.

	Mr. Nicholls reads and enjoys both 'Jane Eyre' and 'Shirley' in which he is portrayed.
19 Jan.	Ellen Nussey returns home.
	Charlotte writes to G. H. Lewes complaining of his unfavourable review of 'Shirley' in the Edinburgh Review.
3 Feb.	Martha Brown tells Charlotte that she has just heard that she had written two books.
c10/11 Feb.	Patrick gives Charlotte her mother's letters and papers to read. She is deeply moved by them.
16 Feb.	Charlotte writes to Ellen Nussey about her mother's letters.
1 Mar. (Fri.)	Charlotte is visited at the Parsonage by Sir James Kay-Shuttleworth of Gawthorpe Hall, trying to persuade her to stay with him, she having already declined two written invitations.
6-9 Mar.	Charlotte stays with Sir James and Lady Kay-Shuttleworth at Gawthorpe Hall, Padiham.
Apr.	Much illness in Haworth generally. All at the Parsonage are unwell and Patrick has bronchitis.
	Patrick instigates enquiries into the water supply.
18 Apr.	Charlotte visits Ellen Nussey, who is ill.
23 Apr.	Death of William Wordsworth.
End Apr.	Patrick, Charlotte and Martha Brown are all ill and Charlotte cancels a visit to London with the Kay-Shuttleworths. The trip is rearranged for May.
18 May	The rearranged trip to London is cancelled due to the illness of Sir James Kay-Shuttleworth.
30 May (Thurs.)	Charlotte leaves on a long trip to London, Edinburgh and Ellen Nussey's home.
30 May-	Stays in London. Visits the Royal Academy and

25 June	sees the Duke of Wellington, her childhood hero. On 12 June she has dinner with Thackeray. Sits for a portrait by George Richmond.
25 June- 3 July	Stays with Ellen Nussey at Brookroyd.
3-6 July	Visits Edinburgh with George Smith and his family.
6-15 July	Stays with Ellen Nussey at Brookroyd. Charlotte is unwell.
15 July	Charlotte returns home. Patrick very worried about her long absence.
	During Charlotte's absence the Parsonage has been re-roofed and redecorated.
End-July	Charlotte's portrait by Richmond and a portrait of the Duke of Wellington arrive at the Parsonage as a gift from George Smith.
18-25 Aug.	Charlotte stays with Sir James and Lady Kay-Shuttleworth at Briery Close, Bowness in the Lake District and there meets Mrs. Gaskell for the first time (19 Aug.). Only bad weather prevents them driving to Coniston to meet the Tennysons.
25 Aug.	Mrs. Gaskell writes to Catherine Winkworth reporting on her first meeting with Charlotte.
Sept.	Patrick again ill with bronchitis.
c25 Sept.	Mrs. Gaskell writes to Charlotte, enclosing some wild flowers (her first letter to her personally).
28 Sept.	Charlotte sends a copy of the 'Poems' by Currer, Ellis and Acton Bell to Mrs. Gaskell.
Sept. / Oct.	Charlotte revising part of 'Wuthering Heights' for its reprint in a single volume with 'Agnes Grey' by Smith, Elder & Company. She gets very upset dealing with her sisters' papers.
Oct.	Charlotte writes the introduction to the new edition of 'Wuthering Heights' and 'Agnes Grey'.

Early Dec.	Charlotte declines an invitation from Mrs. Gaskell to stay with friends at Crix near Chelmsford (letter of refusal 13 December).
10 Dec.	Publication by Smith, Elder & Company of 'Wuthering Heights' and 'Agnes Grey' in a single volume with a preface by Charlotte, the copyright having been purchased from T. C. Newby.
16-23 Dec.	Charlotte goes to stay with Harriet Martineau at 'The Knoll', Ambleside. Whilst there they dine with Edward Quillinan (Wordsworth's son-in-law) on 16 December with Sir James Kay-Shuttleworth on 19 December and with Matthew Arnold on 21 December.
23-26 Dec.	Charlotte stays with Ellen Nussey before returning to Haworth.

1851

28 Jan.	Leyland, Branwell's friend, dies a bankrupt in Manor Gaol.
Feb.	John Stores Smith visits Charlotte at the Parsonage.
5 Feb.	Charlotte declines an invitation from George Smith to visit London. She also declines his invitation to join him, his mother and sisters on a trip to the Rhine in the summer (trip subsequently cancelled).
c7-21 Mar.	Ellen Nussey stays at the Parsonage.
21 Mar.	Charlotte learns from George Smith that James Taylor, with whom she has been in regular contact, is going to live in Bombay.
4 Apr.	James Taylor visits Charlotte at the Parsonage and indicates his interest in marrying Charlotte. Patrick thinks a prospective union, deferred for 5 years, desirable.
12 Apr.	Charlotte asks Ellen Nussey to get her a black and white lace cloak and some chemisettes.

May	Death of Ellen Nussey's dog, 'Flossy Junior'.
	Charlotte goes shopping in Leeds.
21 May	Patrick tells Charlotte that if she marries and leaves him, he will go into lodgings.
28 May (Wed.)	Charlotte goes to London and stays with George Smith and his family.
29 May / 12/19/26 June	Charlotte attends a series of lectures by Thackeray. On the first occasion he introduces her to his mother as 'Jane Eyre', much to her annoyance.
30 May	Thackeray calls on Charlotte. They are disturbed by George Smith who hears her upbraiding him for calling her 'Jane Eyre' the previous evening.
June	Charlotte visits the Great Exhibition at the Crystal Palace. She also visits Dr. J. P. Browne, the phrenologist, in the company of George Smith.
1 June	Charlotte hears D'Aubigne, the French Protestant, preach.
7 June	Charlotte goes to St. James Theatre to see the French actress Rachel in 'Adrienne Lecouvreur' by Scribe.
12 June	Charlotte visits Thackeray and there meets Thomas Carlyle and other literary figures.
16 June	Charlotte goes to hear Cardinal Wiseman preach.
21 June	Charlotte again goes to see Rachel - this time as Camille in 'Les Trois Horaces' by Corneille.
22 June	Charlotte attends a confirmation service at the Spanish Ambassador's chapel at which Cardinal Wiseman officiates.
25 June	George Smith takes Charlotte to Richmond.
27 June	Charlotte leaves London and spends three days with Mrs. Gaskell at her home in Plymouth Grove, Manchester.

30 June	Charlotte returns to Haworth.
July	Ellen Nussey stays at the Parsonage.
27 July	Mr. Nicholls has tea with Charlotte prior to him going to Ireland.
Sept.	William Morgan stays at the Parsonage.
	Thomas Brontë Branwell, Charlotte's cousin and son of Charlotte and Joseph Branwell, visits the Parsonage.
29 Sept.- *8 Oct.*	Margaret Wooler stays at the Parsonage.
Nov.	Charlotte starts work on 'Villette'.
6 Nov.	Charlotte declines an invitation to visit Mrs. Gaskell because of 'neuralgic headache' which frequently affects her.
Nov. / Dec.	Charlotte suffering from jaundice.
1 Dec.	Emily's dog 'Keeper' dies.
Early *Dec.*	Charlotte suffering from influenza and headaches.
17 Dec.	Charlotte, suffering from a bad cold, liver troubles and jaundice, asks Ellen Nussey to come.
19-29 *Dec.*	Ellen Nussey stays at the Parsonage to help Charlotte over her illness.
27 Dec.	Death of Sir Edward Dolman Scott (see 8 November 1848).

1852

Early *Jan.*	Charlotte still very ill. Unable to bend or take solid food.
27 Jan.- *3 Feb.*	Charlotte stays with Ellen Nussey to recuperate.

Haworth from the air, probably in the late 1940s. *(Aero Pictorial)*

29 Jan.	George Smith visits Haworth to see Charlotte because her next book is taking so long but misses her because she is at Brookroyd with Ellen Nussey.
Jan.- *Aug.*	Charlotte generally depressed but finally pulls herself together and starts writing again. On several occasions she writes to James Taylor in India but has no reply.
Late Feb. / *Mar.*	Charlotte better but still suffering from headaches.
Mar.	Patrick ill with bronchitis and Charlotte cancels a planned visit to Sussex with Ellen Nussey.
Late *May /* *Early* *June*	Charlotte goes alone to Filey for a holiday to recuperate from her unhealthy winter. She visits Scarborough to ensure that Anne's tombstone has been properly erected.
June / *July*	Patrick unwell and there are fears that he might lose his sight permanently.
Aug.	Tabby unwell. Patrick suffering badly from inflammation of his right eye. Charlotte finally feels well enough to resume writing 'Villette'.
14 Sept.	Death of the Duke of Wellington.
15-22 *Oct.*	Ellen Nussey spends a week at the Parsonage.
30 Oct.	Charlotte sends part of 'Villette' (about three quarters) to Smith, Elder & Company.
20 Nov.	Charlotte sends the last part of 'Villette' to the publishers.
24 Nov.- *8 Dec.*	Charlotte stays with Ellen Nussey at Brookroyd.

13 Dec. (Mon.)	Mr. Nicholls proposes to Charlotte, who agrees to think it over. Patrick is violently opposed to the idea.
14 Dec.	Charlotte writes to Mr. Nicholls refusing him.
Late-Dec.	Mr. Nicholls offers to resign his curacy but stays on condition marriage is never mentioned.
	Patrick encourages Charlotte to go on a visit to London.

1853

5 Jan.	Charlotte goes to stay with Mrs. Smith in London. Whilst there she corrects the proofs of 'Villette' and visits Newgate and Pentonville Prisons, the Foundling and Bethlehem Hospitals, the Bank of England, the Exchange and Rothschilds.
	Patrick writes to her as 'Flossy'.
28 Jan.	'Villette' is published.
	Mr. Nicholls applies to be a missionary in Australia.
31 Jan.	Patrick writes a reference for Mr. Nicholl's application.
2 Feb.	Charlotte leaves London, meets Ellen Nussey at Keighley and together they return to Haworth.
3 Feb.	Poor review of 'Villette' by Harriet Martineau is published and as a result she and Charlotte fall out.
25 Feb.	An engraving of Thackeray's portrait by Lawrence is delivered to the Parsonage, a gift from George Smith.
Early Mar.	The Bishop of Ripon stays one night at the Parsonage. Mr. Nicholls apparently very depressed.
Late Mar.	Mr. Nicholls is offered a curacy at Kirk Smeaton, near Pontefract.
1 Apr.	Mr. Nicholls temporarily withdraws his application to be a missionary giving rheumatism as an excuse.

22-29 *Apr.*	Charlotte stays with Mrs. Gaskell at Manchester and with Ellen Nussey on her way home.
15 May	Mr. Nicholls breaks down with emotion during the Whit Sunday service whilst giving Charlotte communion for the last time.
27 May (Mon.)	Mr. Nicholls leaves Haworth to become curate at Kirk Smeaton.
May / *June*	Charlotte suffers from a severe attack of influenza and a proposed visit by Mrs. Gaskell is postponed.
	During this time Charlotte starts writing 'Willie Ellin' (unfinished).
June	Patrick ill with eye problems.
July	Mr. Nicholls writes the first of six letters between now and October asking Charlotte to write to him. She finally does so in October.
Aug.	Charlotte goes with Joe Taylor, his wife and baby to Kirkcudbright. The holiday is cut short because of the baby's illness.
11 Aug.	Mr. Nicholls commences his curacy at Kirk Smeaton.
13 Sept.	Charlotte stays with Miss Wooler at Ilkley.
19-23 *Sept.*	Mrs. Gaskell stays with Charlotte at Haworth.
Late Sept.- *6 Oct.*	Charlotte stays with Ellen Nussey at Brookroyd and then with Margaret Wooler at Hornsea.
Oct.	Charlotte meets Mr. Nicholls, now staying with Mr. Grant at Oxenhope.
Nov.	Charlotte, now meeting Mr. Nicholls regularly, cancels a planned visit to London.
27 Nov.	Charlotte starts writing 'Emma' (unfinished).

1854

Jan.   Unbeknown to her father, Charlotte continues to meet Mr. Nicholls.

Feb.   Charlotte tells her father she has been seeing Mr. Nicholls.

11 Feb.   George Smith marries Miss Elizabeth Blakeway.

21 Feb.   Patrick says he is too old to meet a deputation from the Church Pastoral Aid Society.

     First signature of Patrick as 'P. Brontë', having previously used 'P. Bronte'.

28 Mar.   Charlotte writes to Ellen Nussey and by mistake leaves a note to Mr. Nicholls in it.

Late Mar.   Patrick ill with bronchitis.

3 Apr.   Mr. Nicholls comes to the Parsonage and Charlotte's engagement to him is agreed.

11 Apr.   Charlotte writes to tell Ellen Nussey of her engagement.

12 Apr.   Charlotte writes to tell Miss Wooler of her engagement.

1-4 May   Charlotte stays with Mrs. Gaskell in Manchester.

4-13 May   Charlotte goes to Leeds to shop for her trousseau, then visits Joe Taylor and finally stays with Ellen Nussey.

23 May   Mr. Nicholls returns to Haworth to live.

11 June   Mr. Nicholls resigns his curacy at Kirk Smeaton.

16 June   Charlotte writes to Ellen Nussey and Miss Wooler with details of her wedding which is to take place on 29 June.

28 June (Wed.)   Ellen Nussey and Miss Wooler arrive at Haworth for the wedding.

(Evening)   Patrick tells Charlotte that he is feeling too unwell to give her away at her wedding, but in fact he is afraid at

being separated from his last child and of her ability to be able to cope physically with pregnancy, in view of her diminutive size.

29 June (Thurs.)	Marriage of Charlotte to the Rev. Arthur Bell Nicholls at Haworth Church at 8 a.m. She is given away by Miss Wooler and married by Rev. Sutcliffe Sowden. Ellen Nussey is the only other guest.
30 June	Charlotte and Mr. Nicholls leave on their honeymoon, initially to Bangor, Wales.
3 July	They cross to Ireland.
4 July	They arrive at Dublin.
7 July	Charlotte and Mr. Nicholls leave Dublin for Banagher and stay at the Nicholls family home, Cuba House.
15 July	They tour through Western Ireland - Kilkee, Tarbert, Tralee, Killarney and Cork.
c27 July	Charlotte is thrown from her horse.
28 July	They return to Dublin and onto the ferry.
1 Aug. (Tues.)	Charlotte and Mr. Nicholls return to Haworth.
Early Aug.	Rev. Sutcliffe Sowden comes to the Parsonage. Charlotte has plans to marry him off to Ellen Nussey, if possible.
21 Sept.	Mr. Nicholls officially relicensed as curate at Haworth.
Sept./ Oct.	First Ellen Nussey, then Mr. & Mrs. Joe Taylor stay at the Parsonage. Mrs. Gaskell was to have visited but was prevented at the last minute.
10 Oct.	Mr. Nicholls asks Ellen Nussey to burn Charlotte's old letters to her.
31 Oct.	Mr. Nicholls insists on the above.
6 Nov.	Rev. Sutcliffe Sowden and his brother George visit the Parsonage and stay overnight.

8 Nov.	Ellen Nussey finally agrees to burn Charlotte's letters, but does not do so.
11 Nov.	Sir James Kay-Shuttleworth stays for two or three days at the Parsonage and offers Mr. Nicholls the living of Padiham, near Gawthorpe Hall, which is declined as he has promised to remain with Patrick.
28 Nov.	Charlotte and Mr. Nicholls are caught in a storm on the moors. Charlotte then suffers from a sore throat and cold and a general deterioration in her health commences.
Early Dec.	'Flossy', Anne's dog, dies. Charlotte has to cancel a planned visit to Ellen Nussey as there is typhoid in the area. The visit is rearranged for January.

1855

Early Jan.	Charlotte and her husband spend two or three days with Sir James Kay-Shuttleworth at Gawthorpe and she catches cold again after walking in wet grass with thin shoes on.
17 Jan.	Charlotte makes her will, leaving everything to Mr. Nicholls. Charlotte suffering from nausea and faintness. Her visit to Ellen Nussey is cancelled.
30 Jan.	A doctor comes to see Charlotte and determines that she is pregnant.
15 Feb.	Charlotte writes to Laetitia Wheelwright and describes 'No kinder, better husband than mine, it seems to me, there can be in the world.' Her condition deteriorates.
17 Feb.	Tabitha Aykroyd (Tabby) dies.
21 Feb.	Tabitha Aykroyd's funeral.
Mid-Feb.	Patrick ill with bronchitis

Charlotte now too ill to write. Her last letter is to Amelia Taylor, Joe Taylor's wife, with whom she regularly corresponded and thanks her for sending some medicines, which had no effect.

Early Mar. — Sudden improvement in Charlotte's condition.

Mid-Mar. — Charlotte suffers a relapse.

20 Mar. — Patrick writes to Ellen Nussey that Charlotte is close to death.

c21 Mar. — Charlotte becomes delirious.

31 Mar. (Sat.) — Charlotte dies. Cause of death given as phthisis (consumption).

Modern opinion is that it was exhaustion from sickness during pregnancy.

4 Apr. (Wed.) — Charlotte's funeral at which Rev. Sutcliffe Sowden officiates.

5 Apr. — Patrick writes to tell Mrs. Gaskell of Charlotte's death.

8 Apr. (Sun.) — Charlotte's funeral sermon preached by Rev. Dr. Cartman.

13 Apr. — Patrick buys a new dog – a Newfoundland cross terrier which he calls 'Cato'. Later buys another he calls 'Plato'.

16 June — Patrick writes to ask Mrs. Gaskell to undertake a short biography to counteract the many false stories of Charlotte's life then circulating.

23 July (Mon.) — Mrs. Gaskell, together with Catherine Winkworth, visits Patrick at Haworth to discuss the biography. Mr. Nicholls is against the idea.

10 Aug. (Fri.) — Death of John Brown.

13 Aug. — John Brown's funeral conducted by Rev. Nicholls.

1856

July　　Rev. William Gaskell (Mrs. Gaskell's husband) sends a copy of his sermon preached on 4 May at Cross St. Chapel, Manchester to Patrick.

23 July　　Mrs. Gaskell and Sir James Kay-Shuttleworth visit Patrick and Mr. Nicholls at Haworth and take away a number of minute writings done when the Brontës were children.

July /
Aug.　　Mrs. Gaskell visits Brussels. Mdme. Heger refuses to see her but she sees M. Heger and is shown Charlotte's letters to him.

9 Dec.　　Thackeray writes to Patrick from Bradford where he was lecturing.

1857

7 Feb.　　Mrs. Gaskell finishes her biography of Charlotte.

Feb. /
Mar.　　George Smith and Mrs. Gaskell send Patrick some biographical books.

25 Mar.
(Wed.)　　Publication of Mrs. Elizabeth Gaskell's 'Life of Charlotte Brontë'.

2 Apr.　　Patrick writes to Mrs. Gaskell about the 'few trifling mistakes' in the biography.

Early
May　　Lady Scott (formerly Mrs. Robinson) and Rev. Carus Wilson, both threaten Mrs. Gaskell with a libel action because of various allegations in her book.

All unsold copies of the biography are withdrawn for amendment.

26 May　　Mrs. Gaskell issues a retraction of her comments relating to Lady Scott and these are deleted from the 3rd edition.

June　　The Parsonage is painted externally by Humphrey Wood for £1.1.0.

6 June	Charlotte's first book, 'The Professor' is published.
July	Rev. Nicholls sends a series of letters to the Halifax Guardian concerning Cowan Bridge School.
8 July	Francis Leyland visits Patrick at the Parsonage.
17 Aug.	Patrick writes a reference for Nancy and Sarah Garrs to clear them of allegations in Mrs. Gaskell's book.
Sept.	George Smith sends more books to Patrick.

1858

25 Jan.	Dr. Edward White Benson, related to the Sidgwicks of Stonne Gappe, Lothersdale, later to become Archbishop of Canterbury, visits Patrick at the Parsonage.
25 Mar.	Death of Rev. William Morgan, aged 76.
	Completion of a reservoir at Haworth (see 8 August 1849).
15 July	Patrick gives a copy of Charlotte's 'Shirley' to Martha Brown.
Oct.	Patrick gives a copy of Mrs. Gaskell's 'Life of Charlotte Brontë' to Tabitha Brown.

1859

	Mary Taylor returns to England from New Zealand and settles at High Royd, Gomersal.
	Founding of the Yorkshire Penny Bank with Patrick as President of the Haworth Branch.
June	Patrick writes to his niece, Elizabeth Jane Kingston, in Penzance.
19 June	Death of Lady Scott (Mrs. Robinson).
Sept.	Mrs. Gaskell sends a portrait of her husband to Patrick.

1 Dec.	Death of Dr. Crosby (see 1846)
30 Dec.	Death of Rev. Carus Wilson in London.

1860

Apr.	Charlotte's unfinished novel 'Emma' appears in the Cornhill Magazine.
21 July	Patrick's last sermon.
Oct.	Patrick becomes bedridden.
End Oct.	Mrs. Gaskell and her daughter Margaret Emily ('Meta') visit Patrick at the Parsonage.

1861

1 Feb.	Eliza Brown hired to work at the Parsonage.
15 Apr.	Death of Patrick's old friend, John Nunn at Thorndon, Suffolk.
7 June (Fri.)	Patrick dies at 2 p.m. of chronic bronchitis and dyspepsia.
12 June	Patrick's funeral conducted by Rev. Dr. Burnet, Vicar of Bradford. All the shops in Haworth close for the day.
Oct.	Rev. Nicholls resigns his curacy when he is not offered the position of Perpetual Curate at Haworth.
	He returns to Ireland, resigns his clerical orders and becomes a farmer.
	Martha Brown goes with him as a servant and he also takes Patrick's dog 'Plato'.

1862

Aug.	Rev. Nicholls visits Haworth, staying with Mr. Grant at Oxenhope.

1863

25 Mar.   Death of John Greenwood, the Haworth stationer, from whom the sisters used to purchase writing materials. On occasions he would walk to Keighley to buy paper to ensure that he had supplies for them.

1864

25 Aug.   Rev. Nicholls marries his cousin Mary Bell.

Nov.   Trees planted in the graveyard at Haworth Church, previously it was bare.

1865

12 Nov.   Death of Mrs. Elizabeth Gaskell.

Haworth lanes equipped with gas lamps.

1866

Death of Mrs. Mary Sibree (nee Burder) (see 1806).

End Apr.   Death of Patrick's old dog 'Plato'.

1867

8 June   Article appears in the Halifax Guardian suggesting Branwell wrote 'Wuthering Heights'.

Death of Henry Nussey in the south of France.

1869

4 Feb.   Death of Edmund Robinson - drowned in River Ure whilst foxhunting (see 1845).

1874

29 Apr.   Death of James Taylor in Bombay (see 1851).

1875

Death of William Smith Williams.

1879

Haworth Church (not the tower) demolished and rebuilt.

14 Sept.   Last service in the old church.

1880

19 Jan.   Death of Martha Brown at Haworth
(Mon.)

1885

3 June   Death of Margaret Wooler.

1890

9 Jan.   Death of Mdme. Heger.

Publication of 'Miss Miles' by Mary Taylor.

1893

1 Mar.   Death of Mary Taylor at High Royd, Gomersal,
Yorkshire. She is buried in St. Mary's Churchyard,
Gomersal.

1896

6 May   Death of M. Constantin Heger at 72 Rue Nettoyer,
Brussels.

St. Peter's Church, Birstall, where Ellen Nussey was buried in 1897.
(Chris Sumner)

1897

26 Nov.   Death of Ellen Nussey at Moorlane House, Gomersal.
              She is buried in Birstall Churchyard.

1906

2 Dec.   Death of Arthur Bell Nicholls at Banagher,
(Mon.)   Kings Country, Ireland. His widow finds the painting by
              Branwell of his three sisters, folded up on top of a
              wardrobe.

1910

30 Nov.   Death of Mrs. Tabitha Ratcliffe (nee Brown).

1915

27 May   Death of Mrs. Mary Nicholls (nee Bell), Rev. A. B.
              Nicholls' second wife.

WHO'S WHO

A

'ADELAIDE'	Emily's pet goose.
ANDERTON William	West Yorkshire clergyman who often helped out at Haworth Church.
ARNOLD Matthew	Teacher at Rugby. Later a writer and acquaintance of Charlotte.
ATKINSON Thomas	Patrick Brontë's predecessor at Thornton with whom he exchanges livings. Charlotte's godfather.
AYKROYD Tabitha	'Tabby'. Long-serving servant at the Parsonage 1825-1855.
AYLOTT AND JONES	London publishing firm.

B

BARBER David Rev.	Presbyterian Minister, friend of Wesley, from whom Patrick borrowed books.
BEDFORD	Family at Louseythorn, where Patrick lodged.
BELL Mary Anne	Arthur Nicholls' cousin and second wife.
BENSON Dr. Edward White	Later Archbishop of Canterbury.
BRANWELL Anne	Maria's mother.
BRANWELL Benjamin	Maria's brother, Mayor of Penzance.
BRANWELL Charlotte	Maria's sister. Married on the same day.
BRANWELL Elizabeth	Maria's sister. Aunt Branwell.
BRANWELL Jane	Maria's aunt and wife of Rev. John Fennell.

BRANWELL Maria	Patrick Brontë's wife and mother of the Brontës.
BRANWELL Thomas	Maria's father, a Penzance merchant.
BROWN Eliza	Daughter of John Brown. Employed at the Parsonage in 1861.
BROWN John	Stonemason. Haworth church sexton 1835-1855.
BROWN Martha	Daughter of John Brown. Employed at the Parsonage 1843-1861.
BROWN Tabitha	Daughter of John Brown. Employed at the Parsonage.
BROWN William	Brother of John Brown and his successor as sexton.
BROWNE Dr. J. P.	Phrenologist.
BRUNTY Hugh	Patrick Brontë's father.
BRYCE David	Curate at Colne who proposes to Charlotte in 1839.
BUCKWORTH John	Patrick Brontë's vicar at Dewsbury.
BURDER Mary	Niece of Patrick Brontë's landlady at Wethersfield, Essex, with whom he falls in love.

C

CARLYLE Thomas	Poet and writer.
CARTER E. N.	Married to Miss Susan Wooler.
CARTMAN Dr.	Preached at Charlotte's funeral sermon.
CARTWRIGHT Wm.	Owner of Rawfolds Mill, Liversedge.
'CATO'	Patrick Brontë's dog.

CHARNOCK James	Patrick Brontë's predecessor at Haworth.
CLIBBORN	Linen draper at Banbridge who employed Patrick Brontë as a teenager.
COLERIDGE Hartley	Writer, poet and journalist. Son of Samuel Taylor Coleridge.
COLLINS	One time Haworth curate.
CROSBY Dr.	The Robinson's family doctor.
CROSSE John	Vicar of Bradford.
CURRER Frances Mary Richardson	Patron of Bierley Chapel, Bradford.

D

DAVY Mildred	Patrick Brontë's landlady at Wethersfield, Essex.
De QUINCY Thomas	Writer and journalist. A renowned Greek scholar.
DIXON Family	Cousins of Mary and Martha Taylor and friends of Charlotte's.
DONALD Robert	Weaver to whom Patrick Brontë was apprenticed.
DRURY Isabella	Sister of Rev. Theodore Drury, Rector of Keighley.

E

EVANS Anne	Superintendent at Cowan Bridge School.
EYRE Family	of Hathersage, Derbyshire.

F

FENNELL Jane Branwell	Daughter of John and Jane Fennell. Wife of William Morgan. Cousin of Maria Branwell.
FENNELL John	Maria Brontë's (Branwell) uncle. A school headmaster. Godfather to Branwell and Emily.
FIRTH John	Thornton resident and friend of Patrick Brontë.
FIRTH Elizabeth	Daughter of John. Friend of Patrick and Maria Brontë. Godmother to Elizabeth, Branwell and Anne.
FLETCHER Mary (nee Bosanquet)	Widow of John Wesley's confidante, John Fletcher of Madeley, Shropshire and a great influence in religious circles.
'FLOSSIE'	Anne's pet King Charles Spaniel.
'FLOSSIE JUNIOR'	One of Flossie's pups.
FRANKS James	Husband of Elizabeth Firth. Incumbent at Sowerby Bridge, Halifax, and later at Huddersfield.

G

GARRS Nancy	Sister of Sarah. Servant to the Brontës at Thornton and Haworth.
GARRS Sarah	Sister of Nancy. Servant to the Brontës at Thornton and Haworth.
GASKELL Elizabeth Cleghorn	Novelist of Manchester. Friend of Charlotte and author of 'The Life of Charlotte Brontë'.
GOOCH George	Coachman to the Robinson family.
GRANT Joseph Brett	Incumbent at Oxenhope and formerly curate at Haworth.

Looking down Haworth's Main Street. *(John Edenbrow)*

GREENWOOD John	Stationer at Haworth.
GRUNDY Francis	Railway engineer and friend of Branwell.

H

HARSHAW Andrew (Rev.)	Kinsman of James. Teacher at Ballynafern School who taught classics and mathematics to Patrick Brontë.
HARSHAW James	Kinsman of Andrew. Farmer at Donoughmore.
HEATON Family	of Ponden House and one of the most important Haworth families on whom Emily may have based the Linton family of 'Wuthering Heights'.
HEGER Claire Zoe (nee Parent)	Owner of a school in Brussels.
HEGER Constantin	Husband of Claire. A schoolmaster with whom Charlotte fell in love.
'HERO'	A merlin hawk belonging to Emily.
HUDSON John & Sophia	of Easton, Bridlington, friends of the Nussey family and Charlotte.

I

INGHAM Family	Family of Blake Hall, Mirfield.

J

JENKINS Evan	British chaplain in Brussels.

K

KAY-SHUTTLEWORTH Sir James	Literary patron of Gawthorpe Hall, Padiham, near Burnley.

'KEEPER'	Emily's bull mastiff.
KINGSTON Elizabeth	of Penzance, cousin to the Brontës.

L

LEWES G. H.	Editor of the 'Edinburgh Review'.
LEYLAND Francis	Brother of Joseph. Friend of Branwell.
LEYLAND Joseph B.	Brother of Francis. A sculptor and friend of Branwell.
LOCKHART John G	Editor of the 'Quarterly Review'.

M

MARTINEAU Harriet	Novelist, journalist and writer on economic and social themes. Friend of Charlotte.
McLORY Eleanor (Alice)	Wife of Hugh Brunty. Mother of Patrick Brontë.
McLORY Paddy	Her brother.
MOORE Alexander	Headmaster of Glascar Hill School.
MORGAN William	Husband of Jane Fennell. Fellow curate of Patrick's at Wellington and a lifelong family friend. Godfather of Maria.

N

NEWBY Thomas Cautley	Publisher at Cavendish Square, London.
NICHOLLS Arthur Bell	Curate at Haworth. Married to Charlotte. Orginally of a wealthy Irish family.
NOWELL William	of Dewsbury. Falsely accused of desertion from the Army.

NUNN John	Friend of Patrick Brontë who he first met at Cambridge University.
NUSSEY Ellen	Charlotte's greatest friend who she first met at Roe Head School.
NUSSEY George	Brother of Ellen.
NUSSEY Henry	Brother of Ellen. Proposed to Charlotte in 1839. Later incumbent at Hathersage, Derbyshire.

O

OUTHWAITE Fanny	Daughter of a Bradford doctor and close friend to Elizabeth Firth. Godmother of Anne.

P

PARENT Claire Zoe	See HEGER.
PATCHETT Miss	Principal of Law Hill School.
'PLATO'	Patrick Brontë's dog.
POSTLETHWAITE Family	of Broughton in the Lake District where Branwell was tutor.

R

RATCLIFFE Tabitha	see BROWN.
REDHEAD Samuel	Minister of Horton, then Calverley. Appointed to Haworth but driven out in a dispute over the manner of his appointment.
RICHMOND George	London portrait painter.
ROBERSON Hammond	Canon of York and friend of Patrick Brontë.

ROBINSON Family	of Thorp Green, Little Ouseburn to whom Anne was governess and Branwell later became tutor. Branwell formed an association of some sort with Mrs. Lydia Robinson.
ROBINSON William	of Leeds. Portrait painter who gave the Brontë children lessons.

S

SCOTT Sir Edward	Member of Parliament for Lichfield from 1831-1837, related to Mrs. Lydia Robinson and became her second husband.
SCOTT Sir Walter	Romantic writer much admired by the Brontës.
SIBREE Mary	see BURDER.
SIDGWICK Family	of Stonegappe, Lothersdale where Charlotte was governess in 1839.
SIMEON Rev. Charles	Methodist at Cambridge.
SMITH George	Senior partner of Charlotte's publishing firm, Smith, Elder & Company, and a close friend.
SMITH John Stores	London journalist.
SMITH, ELDER & COMPANY	Charlotte's publishers, of Cornhill, London.
SOUTHEY Robert	Poet and historian. Poet Laureate.
SOWDEN Sutcliffe	Vicar of Hebden Bridge and a great friend of Mr. Nicholls, who conducted their wedding and Charlotte's funeral.
STEVENSON ElizabethCleghorn	see GASKELL

T

TAYLOR James	In charge of the clerical staff at Smith,

	Elder & Company. Proposed to Charlotte in 1851.
TAYLOR Joe	Brother of Mary and Martha, of Gomersal, later of Hunsworth Mill, Cleckheaton.
TAYLOR Martha	Younger sister of Mary.
TAYLOR Mary	Lifelong friend of Charlotte, having first met at Roe Head School.
TEALE Dr.	Leeds specialist on lung disease.
TENNYSON Alfred Lord	One of England's greatest poets.
THACKERAY William Makepeace	English journalist, novelist and essayist.
TIGHE Thomas	Rector of Drumgooland and Drumballyroney.
TIGHE William	Half-brother to Thomas, of Rosanna, Co. Wicklow. Great friend of John Wesley.

V

'VICTORIA'	Emily's pet goose.

W

WALKER Amelia	of Lascelles Hall, Huddersfield. Friend of Charlotte who first met her at Roe Head School.
WALKER Frances	Aunt of Amelia. Married to Thomas Atkinson. Godmother to Charlotte.
WEIGHTMAN William	of Appleby, Westmoreland. Curate at Haworth.
WELLINGTON Duke of	British general and military hero. Prime Minister.

WESLEY John	Religious reformer. Founder of Methodism.
WHEELWRIGHT Family	of Finsbury, London. Moved to Brussels and the five daughters attended Pensionnat Heger with Charlotte and Emily. Charlotte particularly friendly with Laetitia.
WHITE Family	of Upperwood House, Rawdon.
WILLIAMS William Smith	Literary adviser and reader to Smith, Elder & Company. He discovered 'Jane Eyre'.
WILSON William Carus	Vicar of Tunstall. Founder of Cowan Bridge School. Writer of children's religious books.
WINKWORTH Catherine	close friend of Mrs. Gaskell and Harriet Martineau.
WOOLER Margaret	Headmistress of Roe Head School and long-time friend of Charlotte.
WORDSWORTH William	Great English poet.

INDICES

.

INDICES

The indices on 'People' and 'Places' refer to all references to them in the book, whilst the 'General' index which follows contains more specific entries only.

PEOPLE

PLACES

GENERAL INDEX